HISTORICAL

EVIDENCE

FOR

UNICORNS

By Larry Brian Radka

153

DEDICATED

To

THE

TRUTH

HISTORICAL EVIDENCE
FOR UNICORNS

By
Larry Brian Radka

— Man Does Not Live By Bread Alone —

Published by:

The Einhorn Press
Post Office Box 3376
Newport, Delaware 19804

ISBN: 0-930401-81-6

LIBRARY OF CONGRESS CATALOG CARD NUMBER: 95-60630

PRICE: Hardcover—$35.00, Softcover—$15.00 (U.S. Currency)

*A NOTE ABOUT THE AUTHOR: On March 22, 1995 a royal proclamation was received from His Royal Highness, Prince Kevin, Prince Regent of Hutt River Principality—announcing that The Honourable Larry Brian Radka has been "nominated for selection as 1994 International Citizen of the Year for Hutt River" by the Heritage Committee of that sovereign state. The appointment is for "Outstanding Service and Selfless Contribution to International Affairs."

NOTABLE HORNS OF UNICORNS

"In the East, at present, horns are used as an ornament for the head, and as a token of eminent rank. (Rosen-müller, 'Morg.' iv 85). The women among the Druses on Mount Lebanon wear on their heads silver horns of native make, 'which are the distinguishing badge of wifehood.' (Bowring's 'Report on Syria,' p. 8)."

"The Popular and Critical Bible Encyclopaedia
and Scriptural Dictionary" — 1912.

"There are at present in the world approximately 600,00 known species of insects, several hundred thousand other invertebrates and nonmammalian vertebrates, and 15,000 mammals. Until comparatively recent times, these were nonexisting, and other species, now extinct, prevailed. Their numbers can not now be estimated, because of the imperfect record which paleontology has thus far disclosed. Nor is the present number complete. Every year adds thousands of newly discovered species to the already hugely swollen list of creatures of the present and the past."

"The Smithsonian Series"

"To regard the Unicorn as wholly fabulous and a product of fancy is an absurd and arbitrary position, and we do well to remember that if the elephant and giraffe and camel should once die out they too, on account of their strange forms, would be thought fabulous."

Joseph Russegger

(The poem on the following page is a slightly modified version, by this author, of Odell Shepard's translation of an old German folk-song.)

THE UNICORN

I stood in the Maytime meadows
   By roses circled round,
Where many a fragile blossom
   Was bright upon the ground;
And as though the roses called them
   And their wild hearts understood,
The little birds were singing
   In the shadows of the wood.

The nightingale among them
   Sang sweet and loud and long,
Until a greater voice than hers
   Rang out above her song;
For suddenly, between the crags,
   Along the narrow vale,
The echoes of a hunting horn
   Came clear upon the gale.

The hunter stood beside me
   Who blew that mighty horn;
I saw that he was hunting
   The gentle unicorn —
But the unicorn is noble,
   He knows his gentle birth,
He knows that God has chosen him
   Above all beasts of earth.

The Unicorn is noble;
   He keeps him safe and high
Upon a narrow path and steep
   Climbing to the sky;
And there no man can take him,
   He scorns the hunter's gun,
By the throne of God the Father
   Rests His only begotten Son.

What would be now the state of us
   But for this Unicorn,
And what would be the fate of us,
   Poor sinners, lost, forlorn?
Oh, may He lead us on and up,
   Unworthy though we be,
Into His Father's kingdom,
   To dwell eternally!

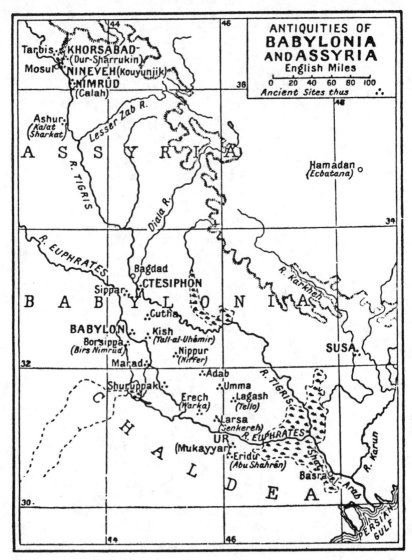

ANTIQUITIES OF
BABYLONIA
AND ASSYRIA
English Miles

This book is written especially for my wife, Wanda, and for my mother, Wanda, both of whom I love dearly. Like Sebastian in "The Tempest," today they have good reasons to say: "Now I will believe that there are unicorns."

I thank those at Baldwin's Book Barn, at West Chester, Pa., who helped me acquire so many old reference books; and a special gratitude is felt for the good spirits who kept inspiring me to write this book.

I

CHAPTER ONE

A N C I E N T   E V I D E N C E

Less than two centuries ago the ancient evidence for the actual existence of unicorns could have been compressed into a few pages, and even these pages would have been a mixture of history and legend. The sparse accounts of these animals which had drifted down to us from the writers of Greece and Rome were intermingled with fable and fiction, and what the Old Testament had to tell us about them was meager and fragmentary.

However, towards the middle of the nineteenth century the proofs of the reality of unicorns began to rise considerably because of the astonishing discoveries made in the newly developing field of archaeology which had sprung up from roots in the Orient. Until then a single case in the British museum was sufficient to hold all the monuments of the early Babylonian and Assyrian civilizations that had flourished thousands of years before. The mummies and other artifacts of Egyptian antiquity scattered throughout the museums of Europe were merely so many curiosities, and the precise nature and age of them were unknown. But, thanks to the skill and patient labor of the pioneers in archaeology: the excavators, language decipherers, and authors — like Sir Austen H. Layard (1817-1894), Sir Henry C. Rawlinson (1810-1895), and George Rawlinson (1812-1902) — the ancient world of the Bible had risen from its forgotten grave to confirm the Scriptures, and the unicorns had risen with it.

These animals are mentioned several times in the Greek as well as the Latin Scriptures; and Odell Shepard says: "In the King James Version of the Bible there are seven clear references to the unicorn, all of which occur in the Old Testament. The animal is mentioned twice in the Pentateuch, once in Job, once in Isaiah, and three times in the Psalms. These passages read as follows: — "

"God brought them out of Egypt; he hath as it were the strength of the unicorn." — Numbers xxiii. 22.

"His glory is like the firstling of his bullock, and his horns are like the horns of unicorns: with them he shall push the people together to the ends of the earth." — Deuteronomy xxxiii. 17.

"Save me from the lion's mouth; for thou hast heard me from the horns of unicorns." — Psalm xxii. 21.

"He maketh them also to skip like a calf; Lebanon and Sirion like a young unicorn." — Psalm xxix. 6.

"But my horn shalt thou exalt like the horn of the unicorn: I shall be anointed with fresh oil." — Psalm xcii. 10.

"And the unicorns shall come down with them, and the bullocks with their bulls; and their land shall be soaked with blood, and their dust made fat with fatness." — Isaiah xxxiv. 7.

"Will the unicorn be willing to serve thee, or abide in thy crib?

"Canst thou bind the unicorn with his band in the furrow? or will he harrow the valleys after thee?

"Wilt thou trust him because his strength is great? or wilt thou leave thy labour to him?

"Wilt thou believe him, that he will bring home thy seed, and gather it into thy barn?" — Job xxxix. 9-12.

"One thing is evident in these passages," adds the authority on unicorns, "they refer to some actual animal of which the several writers had vivid if not clear impressions. Although the allusions were made at widely different times, the characterization is consistent, bringing before us a beast remarkable for strength, ferocity, wildness, and unconquerable spirit. Nothing suggests that it was supernatural, a creature of fancy, for it is linked with the lion, the bullock and the calf; yet it was mysterious enough to inspire a sense of awe, and powerful enough to provide a vigorous metaphor."

THE OLD BABYLONIAN CUNEIFORM WORD FOR UNICORN
(From the Prologue of Hammurabi's Code of Laws)

Notice the word "unicorn" is specifically mentioned twice in the verses Shepard quoted from Job. Some people have long believed that this book tells one of the oldest stories in the Bible. This is because there is no direct reference to the Mosaic legislation in it, and its descriptions and other statements are suited to the period of the patriarchs: as, for instance, the great authority held by old men, the high age of Job, and the fathers offering sacrifices for their families — which suggests it was written before the establishment of the order of Hebrew Priests. Moreover, the author avoided the use of Jehovah, and the scenes took place outside of Palestine. Furthermore, written evidence of a more recent nature has been found in the ancient ruins in the Near East. A record which details a similar story about a fellow like Job has been dug up. And even the old cuneiform Code of Hammurabi has been recovered — in which a match for the puzzling Hebrew word for the biblical unicorn appears.

Cuneiform was a form of writing used extensively in the ancient world, especially by the Babylonians and Assyrians. This system of writing probably originated about four or five thousand years before Christ, with a people of unknown origin. We call them the Sumerians. No doubt, they were blood-related to the Indo-European or Aryan family. Their script gradually developed from a simple picture-type of writing into the more complex types of wedge-script that were used centuries later by the Babylonians and Assyrians. A good example of a later form is shown above. By the fifteenth century B.C. cuneiform was being used widely in the Near East, especially for international correspondence. It wasn't used after the first century B.C., and its existence remained unknown for almost two thousand years thereafter.

Since clay was then one of the few natural resources in the Mid East to be easily acquired, it became the common

A CHALDEAN CUNEIFORM TABLET WITH UNICORN SIGNATURES

material used for cuneiform writing. The clay tablet was the ordinary form used, but clay cones, cylinders, and prisms also were employed. Royal inscriptions were often engraved on huge stone monuments or inscribed upon the long bas-reliefs that adorned palaces and other important architecture. If a monument had room to write on it, the space was usually filled up with cuneiform characters. The clay tablets, or other commonly used forms, varied in size through the centuries in accordance with the practical need and scribal tradition. A popular form was the oblong tablet like the one shown above. The reed stylus with a rectangular or triangular writing end was the instrument used to make the marks in the moist and soft clay tablets. Later they were dried in the sun or baked in a kiln. Their durability is attested to by the fact they have survived for thousands of years.

The Greek historian Herodotus was struck by the very general use made of seals in the city of Babylon by all classes of people. "Every Babylonian," he wrote, "has a seal." It was often ground into cylindrical form so it could be easily rolled over soft clay: and after drying, it looked much like the clay tablet with the heads of unicorns shown above. It served as a personal symbol to be stamped or rolled on letters, contracts, and other documents used in commercial transactions.

AN EARLY BABYLONIAN PASTORAL SCENE
(On a Seal from around Abraham's Time)

The famous monument on which Hammurabi's Code of Laws is engraved is not made of clay, but of royal diorite. He is generally identified by most Assyriologists with Amraphel of Genesis, King of Shinar, who with Arioch of Ellasar, Cheodorla'oma of Elam and Tidal, King of Goiim, invaded Canaan in the time of Abraham.

The pastoral scene above shows what Abraham was probably preoccupied with when they invaded. On the lower right is a herdsman driving forth, with the crack of his whip, a herd of unicorns from a goat-house. On the lower left a herder, his dog, and some strange-looking animals are out to pasture. Many of Hammurabi's laws were expressly designed to cover this particular occupation.

Hammurabi was the sixth of eleven kings of the Old Babylonian Dynasty ruling Chaldea. He enacted his famous code or "the law of the land" at the very beginning of his reign. His stela was discovered in the winter of 1901-1902 in the acropolis mound at Susa by an expedition sent out by the French government. The inscribed stone is almost eight feet high, and was broken into three pieces which were easily rejoined. On the obverse side is a bas-relief showing King Hammurabi receiving the laws from a multi-horned god sitting on a throne. Sixteen columns of text are engraved below it, four and a half of which form the prologue. A few more columns on this side are missing. They were probably cut off by an Elamite conqueror.

HAMMURABI (C. 2123-2080 BC) RECEIVING LAWS FROM A GOD

The reverse side is complete and carries twenty-eight columns, of which the last five form the epilogue. It is a splendid example of the best archaic cuneiform script, and its nearly 4000 lines of writing make it the longest Babylonian record ever discovered.

The law code has almost 300 decrees, and several deal with domesticated animals, which appear to have been somewhat troublesome. Others fixed the prices charged in business transactions, and some set the amount to be paid in damages for various crimes. These laws are often similar to, but sometimes not as severe as, some of the judgments given to Moses in the Book of Exodus. The following translated samples are extracted from Dr. George A. Barton's work entitled "Archaeology and the Bible":

179. If there is a wife of a god, priestess, or sacred harlot, whose father has given her a dowry and written a record of gift; and in the record of gift he has written, "after her she may give it to whomsoever she pleases," and has granted her full discretion; after her father dies she may give it after her to whomsoever she pleases. Her brothers have no claim upon her.

ANCIENT ONE-HORNED DOMESTIC OXEN OF MESOPOTAMIA
(From George Rawlinson's "Five Great Monarchies")

248. If a man hires an ox and breaks off _its horn_, or cuts off its tail or injures the flesh which holds the ring, money to ¼ its value he shall pay.

249. If a man hires an ox and a god strikes it and it dies, the man who hires the ox shall take an oath in the presence of a god and shall go free.

These laws are said to favorably compare with some of the laws given to Moses by Jehovah, and Exodus 21:29 shows there is some basis for this report:

> But if the ox were wont to push with _his horn_ in time past, and it hath been testified to his owner, and he hath not kept him in, but that he hath killed a man or a woman; the ox shall be stoned, and his owner also shall be put to death.

Notice in both Hammurabi's and Mose's laws that the horn on the ox is spoken of as "its" or "his" horn. They must be speaking of one-horned animals like those above, which are often portrayed on the ancient monuments. If so, then Exodus is really the first place in the Bible that calls our attention to a type of unicorn.

It may be surprising to read whom laws 179 and 249 mention, but deities are often spoken of in the Bible. It specifically mentions the gods well over 200 times in the King James Authorized Translation, and they quite obviously weren't all inanimate idols. And the Dead Sea Scrolls are packed with gods — the walking, talking, human types. And after all, Malachi, the last book of the

ONE AND TWO-HORNED OXEN, FROM BABYLONIAN CYLINDERS
(From Rawlinson's "Five Great Monarchies")

Old Testament, even says that Judah had profaned the holiness of the Lord, and married the daughter of a god! And, as my vigilant sister Georgiana explicitly pointed out to me, Habbakuk 3:3 says: "God came from Temen."

Temen is located in the Middle East, near Mount Sinai. It is hard to fathom God the Father rising out of a desert on this dinky planet, but it is conceivable that just before the Flood, the Lord God took pity on his frightened children, "the gods cowered like dogs" — all humbled, and weeping, and allowed some to survive, and drift down later into Temen. The Babylonian scriptures just cited fully affirm that some deities did remain in the flesh, in spite of their sins, and the Bible hardly denies it. (Read of those who knew the Godhead, in Romans 1:18-32.) After all, the rampant evil perpetrated by sons of God, along with that of their charges, the sons and daughters of men, is what caused the Flood, as Gen. 6:1-5 says:

> And it came to pass, when men began to multiply on the face of the earth, and daughters were born unto them, that the sons of God saw the daughters of men that they were fair; and they took them wives of all which they chose. And the LORD said, My spirit shall not always strive with man, for that he also is flesh: yet his days shall be an hundred and twenty years. There were giants in the earth in those days; and also after that, when the sons of God came in unto the daughters of men, and they bare children to them, and the same became mighty men which were of old, men of renown.
>
> And GOD saw that the wickedness of man was great in the earth, and that every imagination of the thoughts of his heart was only evil continually.

This makes it clear the sons of God (or gods) were also in the flesh. How could they have had children if they were not? And one of the reasons the sons of men were so wicked was because many of the gods, their teachers, were so wicked! In "The Babylonian Genesis," Alexander Heidel says: "The gods not only had human forms and were clothed in garments which differed very little from human dress, but also had human needs (requiring food, drink, sleep, etc.) and were guilty of human misconduct." He compares the Babylonian gods with a quote from Cicero, who is referring to the poets of Greece and Rome:

> The poets have represented the gods as inflamed by anger and maddened by lust, and have displayed to our gaze their wars and battles, their fights and wounds, their hatreds, enmities and quarrels, their births and deaths, their complaints and lamentations, the utter and unbridled license of their passions, their adulteries and imprisonments, their unions with human beings and the birth of mortal progeny from an immortal parent.

As we see, the Flood had taught many of the gods absolutely nothing. Some were still as evil as ever, and many of their divine mates, the goddesses, were just as deviant. In his "Records of the Ancient Past," A. H. Sayce, a noted English divine and Oxford professor of Assyriology, included a good piece of evidence that attests to the fact that they mixed with royalty and spawned some of the ancient kings. He quotes the record of an endowment made by Semitic King Sin-gashid (c. 2600 B.C.) of Akkad to the Temple E-ana ("House of heaven"). The 27 lines of Akkadian Cuneiform inscribed on the artifact, which was meticulously copied from an earlier record that has been traced to the tower of Babel, were translated by Theo. G. Pinches, a curator in the British Museum, as follows:

> Sin-gashid, king of ERECH, king of AMNANUM, and patron of E-ANA, to LUGAL-BANDA his god and NIN-GUL his goddess. When he built E-ANA he erected E-KANKAL, the house which is the seat of the joy of his heart. During his dominion he will endow it with 30 "gur" of wheat, 12 "manna" of wool, 10 "manna" of produce, 18 "qa" of oil according to the tariff, and 1 shekel of gold. May his years be years of plenty.

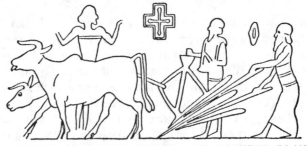

AN ANCIENT SUMERIAN SEEDER, OR MACHINE PLANTER
(From Dr. Breasted's "Conquest of Civilization")

The gods had to eat; so the tariff had to be paid, but what is really significant about all this is what Sayce further informs us of. He says that "it is to be noted that the inscription is dedicated to a god and a goddess whose names I provisionally transcribe as 'Lugal-banda' ('powerful king,' or 'king of youthful strength') and 'Nin-gul,' his consort (as we learn from the second volume of the 'Cuneiform Inscriptions of Western Asia,' pl. 59, II. 24 and 25)." He says that "this identification of Ningul as the consort of Lugal-banda is important," and that it shows that Sin-gashid "calls her his mother, and himself her son." In other words, King Sin-gashid was the child of an earthly father and heavenly mother! He also says that the late George Smith, who deciphered a famous Babylonian account of the Deluge, refers to her as "the earliest known queen in the Euphrates valley."

Perhaps the most important feature of Hammurabi's Code of Laws, which originated, like the Creation and Flood records, in ancient Sumer, is that it uses the Hebrew equivalent of that puzzling word rendered in the King James Bible as "unicorn." The Hebrew word is spelled in English in several ways, such as "rim," raim," "reem," "re êm," and so on — of which "rim" appears to be one of the most popular. It is essentially identical to the Babylonian word which comes from a language much older than the Hebrew. In line seven of column three in the prologue of Hammurabi's Laws, the word in cuneiform is translated into English from the transliteration of Dr. Robert Francis Harper as "Rîmu," which has been identified as the same as the Hebrew word "Rim" which eventually translated into the English Bible as "Unicorn."

ANCIENT EVIDENCE

James Henry Breasted, the famous American historian, Orientalist, and archaeologist, said the picture with the seeder on the previous page was carved on a small stone seal. In his book "Ancient Times" he indicates these men were from Sumer by inserting the illustration between his text on the "Rise of Sumerian Civilization." We see two men operating a seeder and plow. One is feeding grain into the funnel which allows the seed to fall down through a tube toward the blade of the plow and on down into the freshly cut furrow. The other man to the right is maneuvering the plow while a third steers the yoke of unicorns pulling the device. It may, on first thought, seem a little strange that unicorns are being worked instead of two-horned oxen, but the Bible tells us that out of the whirlwind the LORD challenged Job's ability to do the very same things with the unicorn as these men are doing. The LORD suggested that the unicorn could be tamed (indicating he was not, at that time); and the drawing above aptly demonstrates that a primitive ox-type of unicorn was domesticated; so Job must have lived before the time of these ancient Sumerians.

But the really strange things about this very unusual artifact are the familiar symbols appearing in the sky behind the heads of the unicorns. In his work on ancient Mesopotamia, Rawlinson included a drawing of "a double lozenge" and also a double cross ("often repeated three times") on the artifacts dug up there. Dr. Breasted is quoted as saying he found "Messianism a thousand years before its appearance among the Hebrews," His illustration undoubtedly presents a very good example. The cross alone, which symbolizes the coming of Christ, shows that the belief in a Savior was around a long before the Jews and Christians found out about Jesus; but if we unite this symbol of Christ to the spiritual sign appearing in the sky behind it, the unification suggests that these hump-backed unicorns had already received the humble spirit of Jesus, which would have inspired these poor animals to gently bear their burden. So perhaps a thousand years before Moses's time, God had already bound some types of unicorns. If Job was living in the time of Moses, then the LORD'S questions directed at Job's abil-

MORE ONE-HORNED OXEN FROM MESOPOTAMIA
(From Rawlinson's "Five Great Monarhcies")

ity to make the unicorn serve him would have been irrel-
evant. This line of reasoning firmly places Job pretty
far back into the past — long before Moses could have
even thought of bringing the Scriptures to Israel.

For those who still might not be convinced that the
story of Job did not originate with Moses, who is believed to have written several books of the Old Testament, we would like to point out that Abraham was a very
educated man who came from a priestly family. According
to Josephus, the Jewish historian, who lived around the
time of Christ, he taught Babylonian astronomy and mathematics to the Egyptian priests during his sojourn in
their country. He probably also taught them the story
of Job. Moses was born in Egypt, raised up in the royal
court, and taught by Egyptian priests. It doesn't take a
great imagination to see how he got the story of Job,
whose attributes and circumstances, added to the following evidence of tamed Sumerian unicorns, should firmly
place him back beyond the cradle of civilization.

And to give us an idea of just how old Sumer or Sumeria
really is, we'll refer to Sheldon Cheney. In his "World
History of Art" he includes a photograph of two friezes
recovered by the British Museum and the University of
Pennsylvania, dating to about 3100 B.C., on which appear
several domestic unicorns standing near some relaxing
Sumerians. Speaking of the great English archaeologist
who dug up the remains of Abraham's city of Ur, he says:

A SUMERIAN MULTI-HORNED GOD
(From Sir J. A. Aammerton's "Wonders of the Past")

Professor C. Leonard Woolley, who had done more than any other, as archaeologist and writer, to dig the Sumerians out of obscurity and place them prominently in the first episode of the pageant of human civilization, is willing to give them precedence over the once vaunted Akkadians or true Babylonians as founders of Asiatic civilization. He then goes further, to place them before the Egyptians, as pioneer lawgivers, as inventors, and as artists. He points out that in the period when the communities of Sumeria were flourishing, say from 3500 B.C., Egypt still had no metals, had no not invented or discovered the potter's wheel, and owned no written language.

Above is a Sumerian god with a measuring rod, cord, and adze. He is giving directions for building another great ziggurat and shrine. Before him is Ur-Engur, founder of the third and last dynasty of Ur. Their city-nation was destroyed a few centuries later, about the time Abraham left. He bears more horns than Hammurabi's god because he was older, and had more knowledge and power. As time went on, the wars of the gods went on, and their flesh perished; so much divine knowledge and power left Earth, or was buried in the rubble. Their progeny learned less, and knew less, and therefore had less power; so they had to bear less horns. And Jesus Christ was the very last,

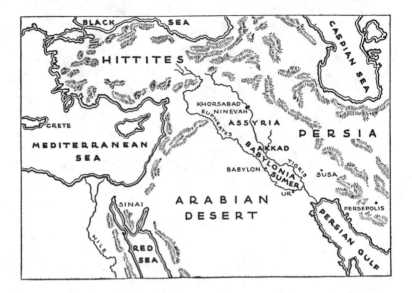

A MAP OF THE ANCIENT NEAR EAST

and the only begotten Son of God. And like the Unicorn, He bore only one — the Horn of our Salvation!

The Egyptian civilization, like the Sumerian that it followed, also verified the existence of certain types of domestic unicorns, as we can very easily determine by just glancing at the illustration on the following page. And just like the Sumerians, they used a type of picture-writing known as "hieroglyphics" (sacred sculptures) which later evolved into an altered and abbreviated form called "hieratic" (priestly) writing in which most formal Egyptian literature is written. Beside being literate, they had a keen artistic talent for painting vivid autobiographies on the walls of their tombs. Some of these burial chambers were cut out of walls of solid rock, with no outward ornamentation on them whatsoever. But the interiors were often gayly painted with scenes from every-day life. Some of these, the tombs of Beni Hassan, located East of the Nile in Middle Egypt, were discovered because they had not been concealed, as was the normal custom. A brief description of these tombs is given in "Barnes General History," which imparts that "a recent visitor to these tombs writes:"

ANCIENT EVIDENCE

EGYPTIANS SLAUGHTERING A UNICORN
(From George Rawlinson's "History of Herodotus")

Having ascended the broad road which leads gradually
up to the entrances, we found ourselves on a sort of
platform cut in the cliff nearly half-way to the top,
and saw before us about thirty high and wide doorways, each leading into one chamber or more, excavated in the solid rock. The first we entered was a large
square room, with an open pit at one end, — the mum-
my-pit; and every inch of the walls was covered with
pictures. Coming into this tomb was like getting hold
of a very old picture-book, which said in the beginning, "Open me and I will tell you what people did
a long time ago." Every group of figures told a separate story, and one could pass on from group to group
till a whole life was unfolded. Whenever we could
find a spot where the painted plaster had not been
blackened or roughened, we were surprised at the
variety of the colors, — delicate lilacs and vivid
crimsons and many shades of green.

"Though these pictures on the walls of tombs were supposed to serve the dead," says this old history book,
"they were no less representations of real life. Were it
not for them, we should never have learned the secrets
of those homes along the Nile where people lived, loved,
and died over four thousand years ago."

The drawing we will see of an Egyptian tomb-painting
on the next page was put out for "Bible Students." It
represents real life also. We rescued it from the back
of an old edition of the King James Translation of the
Bible printed by the Oxford University Press in March
of 1896. The representatives of the British Museum, Sir
Edward M. Thompson, the Principal Librarian, and Dr. E.

"STRANGERS COMING INTO EGYPT" (B)

A. Wallis Budge, the Keeper of Egyptian and Assyrian Antiquities, who supplied the description of the wall-painting, identify the unicorn presented by the chief as the oryx, but they don't mention the other one. It has no beard, but does have marks on its horn and other similar features; so it may be a young or female oryx. They say:

This scene occurs in a series of wall-paintings in the tomb of an Egyptian noble at Beni-hasan in Upper Egypt, of the period of the twelfth dynasty, about 2400 B. C. The noble was Khnemu-hetep, administrator of the Eastern desert and prince of the city of Menāt-Khufu, one of whose duties was to receive the tribute of foreigners. The scene represents the arrival of a company of the tribe of the Āmu from the desert. Commencing with the upper division of the picture, Khnemu-hetep, stands on the right facing the royal scribe Nefer-hetep, who holds up an inscription stating that in the sixth year of the king Usertsen II a company of thirty-seven of the Āmu brought an offering of stibium or eye-paint. Behind the scribe is the superintendent of the huntsmen; and then come the foreigners, headed by their chief Abesha presenting an oryx. The men of the party have beards, and the greater number, both men and women, wear garments embroidered or woven in patterns, contrasting with the simple dress of the Egyptians. Among their weapons

"STRANGERS COMING INTO EGYPT" (A)

will be noticed the throwing-stick. This scene re-calls the visit of Jacob's sons to Egypt with their gift of 'a little balm, and a little honey, spices, and myrrh, nuts and almonds' (Genesis 43. 11), for Joseph, 'the lord of the land.'

Above is Part A of this long mural. When assembled in the proper order of viewing, part A (enlarged) is on the right; B (also enlarged) is in the center; and C is on the left. For those not familiar with the particular type of unicorn seen therein, Edward Topsell, an expert on four-footed beasts, offers us this 17th century description:

It is certain that it is of the kind of wild Goats by the description of it, differing in nothing but this, that the hair groweth not like other beasts, falling backward to his hinder parts, but forward toward his head, and so also it is affirmed of the Ethiopian Bull, which some say is the Rhinoceros. They are bred both in Libya and Egypt, and either of both countries yieldeth testimony of their rare and proper quali-ties. In quantity it resembleth a Roe, having a beard under his chin. His colour is white or pale like milk, his mouth black, and some spots are upon his cheeks, his back-bone reacheth to his head, being double, broad, and fat; his horn, standeth upright, black, and so sharp, that they can not be blunted against brass or iron, but pierce through it readily.

"STRANGERS COMING INTO EGYPT" (C)

In his study entitled "The Lore of the Unicorn," Odell Shepard informs us that:

> Samuel Bochart devoted twenty folio pages of amazing erudition to an attempt to prove that both the "Re'-em" and the unicorn derive from the oryx, basing his argument upon a firm belief — for which he had the authority of Aristotle and Pliny — that all oryxes are one-horned.
>
> Professor Martin Lichtenstein of Berlin, a far less learned man but better acquainted with antelopes, supported the oryx theory by citation of Egyptian monuments. He reproduced a mural decoration found in the pyramid at Memphis showing five antelopes, one of them certainly intended as a unicorn, led by human figures, the whole scene representing a ritualistic offering.

Shepard adds that L. Twining, in his "Symbols and Emblems of Early and Mediaeval Christian Art," says the unicorn was "known to the Egyptians and is found among their hieroglyphics." Our own research confirms this; and E. A. Wallis Budge included the sign of the Unicorn (below) in "Gods of the Egyptians." He ties him to the hieroglyphic form of the name Set ('to be appointed'). "In early dynastic times it is tolerably certain that the worship of Set was widespread," but his popularity appeared to suffer greatly "because he was associated with the occupation of Northern Egypt by the Hyksos, who identified him with certain Semitic, Syrian gods." He says his signification "is not so easy to understand because the animal has not yet been identified." He looks a lot like a unicorn:

GODLY EVIDENCE

"Who is like unto thee, O LORD, among the gods?"

— Exodus 15:11.

Ye great gods,
guardians of heaven and earth,
whose onset brings fight and battle;
who have enlarged the dominion of Tiglath-pileser,
the beloved prince,
the desire of your heart, the lofty shepherd;
whom in your faithful heart, ye have called;
whose head ye have crowned with a lofty crown . . .

THE KING'S UNICORN HUNT
(From "The Iconographic Encyclopaedia")

Tiglath-pileser, the powerful king, king of hosts, who has no rival, king of the four quarters (of the world), king of all rulers, lord of lords, king of kings; the lofty prince, to whom, in the name of Shamash, a pure sceptre was given, and who rules over the nations, the subjects of Bel, in their entirety; the legitimate shepherd whose name is exalted above all rulers; the lofty judge whose weapons Ashur has sharpened, and whose name, as ruler over the four quarters of the world, he has proclaimed forever; the conqueror of distant lands, which form the boundaries on north and south; the brilliant day, whose splendour overthrows the world's regions; the terrible, destroying flame, which like the rush of the storm sweeps over the enemy's country . . .

Ashur and the great gods who have enlarged my kingdom, who have given me strength and power as my portion, commanded me to extend the territory of their (the gods') country, putting into my hand their powerful weapons, the cyclone of battle. I subjugated lands and mountains, cities and their rulers, enemies of Ashur, and conquered their territories. With sixty kings I fought, spreading terror, (among them) and achieved a glorious victory over them. A rival in combat, or an adversary in battle, I did not have. To Assyria I added more land, to its people I added more people, enlarging the boundaries of my land and conquering all (neighbouring?) territories.

THE KING'S VICTORY CELEBRATION AFTER THE UNICORN HUNT
(From Rawlinson — a Bas-relief at Calah — Nimrûd)

At that time I marched also against the people of Qummuh, who had become unsubmissive, withholding the tax and tribute due to Ashur, my lord. I conquered Qummuh to its whole extent, and carried off their booty, . . .

I conquered, in all, from the beginning of my rule to the fifth year of my reign, forty-two countries and their princes, from the other side of the Lower Zab, the boundary of far-off mountain forests, unto the other side of the Euphrates to the land of the Hittites and the Upper Sea toward the west. I made them one nation and amalgamated them; took hostages from them and imposed on them taxes and tribute.

I also conducted many other campaigns against enemies who could not approach my military superiority, covering good country in my war chariot and on bad roads pursuing the enemy afoot. Thus I always prevented an inroad of my enemies into my country.

Tiglath-pileser, the valiant hero, who holds a sceptre that has no rival, and who is perfect in the deeds of the battlefield.

The gods Ninib and Nergal had presented my majesty with their mighty weapons and their lofty bow; and at the bidding of Ninib, who loves me, I killed with my mighty bow, my sharp lance of iron, and my arrow, four huge and powerful male wild oxen — (unicorns) — in the prairies of the country of Mitani and near the city of Arazigi, situated east of the land of the Hittites. I brought home to my city Asshur their hides and their horns.

THE KING'S LION HUNT
(From a Bas-relief from Nimrûd — British Museum)

I hunted and killed ten powerful male elephants in the country of Harran and on the banks of the Chaboras. I also captured alive four elephants; and brought the hides and the tusks of the ten, together with the live elephants, to my city Asshur. At the bidding of Ninib, who loves me, with a stout heart, I killed on foot one hundred and twenty lions with courageous attack. From my chariot I slew as many as eight hundred lions; and also laid low as trophies (? of my chase) all kinds of beasts of the field and of winged birds soaring aloft.

After I had thus successfully overcome all the enemies of Ashur, I erected a temple to my lady Ishtar of Asshur; also a temple to Martu, and Bel-Dibbarra; and renovated temples to deities and to gods in my city Asshur, which had become dilapidated, and completed their restoration. I constructed the gateways to these temples and led the great gods, my lords, into them, thus gladdening their divine heart. I rebuilt and restored palaces, my royal residences, in the outlying districts of my country—palaces which in the course of many years during

A MORE SPLENDID SACRIFICE
(A Composite Reproduction)

*the reign of my fathers had been forsaken, had fallen
into decay and were now heaps of ruins. I also rebuilt
the crumbling walls of cities in my country; repaired
the storehouses and granaries throughout the whole of
Assyria and unloaded into them more grain than my fathers
had done, heaping it high. Herds of horses, cattle, and
asses I collected, which in the strength of Ashur, my
lord, my hand had captured as spoil in the lands which
I had conquered. I also caught in the high mountain forests herds of hinds and stags, gazelles and steinbocks
— which Ashur and Ninib, the gods who love me, had given
unto me as the result of my chase. I brought together
whole troops of them, and reckoned their number like
a large herd of small cattle. I sacrificed to Ashur,
my lord, from year to year, kids and lambs, their offspring, together with the more splendid sacrifices, according to my heart's desire. . . .
Written in the month Siwan, the month of the Gemini, on
the 29th day of the month, . . .*

The preceding pages of text in Berlin Italic type consist of excerpts from a prism inscription of eight hundred lines belonging to Assyrian King Tiglath-pileser I
who reigned around 1120 B.C. They were translated by
William Muss-Arnolt, and cover a period of five years of
his reign. This large clay cylinder, over 15 inches high
and very poorly preserved, was discovered in the foundations of his palace at Kalat Sharkat by Hormuzd Rassam,
the chief assistant and successor to Sir A. H. Layard.
It is a very important source of information, and is, in
fact, a good native history.

THE UNICORN: A MORE SPLENDID SACRIFICE
(From George Rawlinson's "Five Great Monarchies")

The sacrificial scene above is copied from an obelisk found at Nimrûd. "This scene is represented on a mutilated obelisk belonging to the time of Asshur-izir-pal," says George Rawlinson, "which is now in the British Museum. The sculptures on this curious monument are still unpublished." Maybe this is because the god sitting on the throne and talking to the priest looks much too real. Nevertheless, since we do better at observing and commenting than we do at writing, we'll let George repeat his description of this curious scene — in which his "bull" displays the unmistakable feature of a unicorn. After first speaking of a monument of the reign of Esarhaddon, he goes on to describe this sacrificial scene:

> With respect to the mode of sacrifice we have only a small amount of information, derived from a very few bas-reliefs. These unite in representing the bull as the special sacrificial animal. In one we simply see a bull brought up to a temple by the king; but in another, which is more elaborate, we seem to have the whole of a sacrificial scene fairly, if not exactly, brought before us. Towards the front of the temple, where the god, recognisable by his horned cap, appears seated upon a throne, with an attendant priest, who is beardless, paying adoration to him, advances a procession consisting of the king and six priests, one of whom carries a cup, while the other five are

THE UNICORN: A MORE SPLENDID SACRIFICE
(From Nimrûd — in the British Museum)

employed about the animal. The king pours a libation over a large bowl, fixed in a stand, immediately in front of a tall fire-altar, from which flames are rising. Close behind this stands the priest with a cup, from which we suppose that the monarch will pour a second libation. Next we observe a bearded priest directly in front of the bull, checking the advance of the animal, which is not to be offered till the libation is over. The bull is also held by a pair of priests, who walk behind him and restrain him with a rope attached to one of his fore-legs a little above the hoof. Another pair of priests, following closely on the footsteps of the first pair, completes the procession: the four seem, from the position of their heads and arms, to be engaged in a solemn chant. It is probable, from the flame upon the altar, that there is to be some burning of the sacrifice; while it is evident, from the altar being of such a small size, that only certain parts of the animal can be consumed upon it. We may conclude therefore that the Assyrian sacrifices resembled those of the classical nations, consisting not of whole burnt offerings, but of a selection of choice parts, regarded as specially pleasing to the gods, which were placed upon the altar and burnt, while the remainder of the victim was consumed by priest or people.

HISTORICAL EVIDENCE FOR UNICORNS

In his work "Ancient Iraq," Dr. Georges Roux, describes a typical Middle Eastern sacrificial scene as follows:

> Every day throughout the year religious ceremonies were performed in the temple: the air vibrated with music, hymns and prayers; bread, cakes, honey, butter, fruit were laid on the god's table; libations of water, wine or beer were poured out into vases; blood flowed on the altar, and the smoke of roasting flesh mixed with the fumes of cedar wood, cyprus-wood or incense filled the sanctuary. The main object of the cult was the service of the gods, the "dullu." The gods were supposed to live a physical life and had daily to be washed, anointed, perfumed, dressed, attired, and fed, the regular supply of food being ensured by "fixed offerings" established once and for all by the king as supreme chief of the clergy, and by pious foundations.

To all of this, added to the evidence other ancient monuments present, we must conclude that the gods who were "supposed to live a physical life," did, in fact, live a very physical life, in bodies just like ours — as the sacrificial scene on the preceding page so plainly confirms. Notice the stack of provisions piled up on the table; and contrary to Rawlinson's description, notice how casually the beardless priest and god amplify their words with hand gestures. This is very natural and very human-like. There's no sign of "adoration" displayed here. They're just conversing like you and I. The king looks like he has just dipped his beaker into the caldron and filled it with a flammable fluid, perhaps a volatile petroleum product or high-proof alcohol, and from that he has filled the shallow vessel from which he is casting the libation into the altar-pot in order to create a more impressive demonstration by making the flames flare up higher. The priest behind him looks like he is patiently waiting for his plate to be filled; and the four following behind him may be smiling and clapping their hands, or snapping their fingers. And the victim, the unicorn, is naturally hesitant to join in their bloody festivity.

CHALDEAN DIVINITIES
(From Rawlinson's "Five Great Monarchies")

Muss-Arnolt's translation says that Tiglath-pileser renovated temples "to deities and to gods." This implies that the king was speaking of two different kinds of entities, or else he was being very redundant. The deities must have been his inanimate idols because the king "led" — not "carried" — the great gods, his lords, into the gateways to the temples. These gods certainly moved some how if they were led; so they must have been alive, and in John 10:34-36 the Master verifies this:

34. Jesus answered them, Is it not written in your law, I said, Ye are gods?
35. If he called them gods, unto whom the word of God came, and the scripture cannot be broken;
36. Say ye of him, whom the Father hath sanctified, and sent into the world, Thou blasphemest; because I said, I am the Son of God?

Three divine personages, found on artifacts assigned to the old Babylonian and Sumerian era, are portrayed at the top of this page. George Rawlinson calls those on the right and left "priests," but since both appear to bear horns and wear the same apparel as the goddess in the center, "gods" might be a better classification. According to the divine emblems engraved on an ancient obelisk stored in the British Museum, horns are telltale signs of the gods. The one on the left holds a trident. Some in the early Christian Church say it is a "disguised cross." Here it may symbolize the Trinity. The divinity on the right holds a "Crux Ansata" which is "a symbol of life" — the promise to be offered by the coming Savior.

"Mitani" (Mitanni on the map), "east of the land of the
Hittites," is where King Tiglath-pileser I killed four
"powerful male wild oxen" (or unicorns). Before the Hittites overran it, this country was long dominated by the
culture and religion of the primordial Aryans of Harri,
a people highly civilized and as old as their relatives,
the ancient Sumerians. Haran is where Abraham sojourned
with his very attractive wife Sarai, who was a Sumerian
princess or goddess. Mari is where the beautiful 4000
year-old statue of a two-horned Caucasian goddess was
found by archaeologists in 1934. Carchemish, northeast
of Aleppo, on the Euphrates, and in the close vicinity
thereof, is where two extraordinary unicorn monuments,
pictured on the next two pages, were discovered. These
sites are very near or well within the ancient borders of
Mitani. All the things just mentioned have a very close
relationship with each other, but the scope and magni-
tude of the subject and the limited space available in
this work prevent further discussion. However, in the
future we hope to cover it thoroughly in another book.

"LORD OF THE BEASTS"
(From "Wonders of the Past")

The custodian above has been accurately identified as
a deity, very much like Adam, who was also himself a god,
or the son of God (Luke 3:38). This ancient memorial,
found in the land that was probably part of the original
Kingdom of Harri, which embraced Mount Ararat, where the
Ark supposedly rested, could very well depict old Adam
— the god who fathered all the generations of promising
sons and daughters. His divine nature was certainly not
forgotten by his children in northern Mesopotamia. This
huge monument portraying the god embracing an ignoble
assembly of animals would hardly be arduously chiseled
out of hard rock unless the event was very meaningful.

The young unicorn shown above, and the one on the next
page, which seems to be checking behind for hunters, are
the same kind later generations of Mesopotamians would
immortalize in ageless stone. They would chisel them in
walls, staircases, columns, entrances, and edifices of
their royal palaces. They endured both time and trou-
ble, to return today to inspire a renewed sense of awe.
Unfortunately, the living species did not fare as well.

But the evidence of their ancient existence did. It is
often endowed with a very subliminal nature, yet it still
quietly speaks out — as the written word so often does.

"NATURALISM IN CARVEN STONE"
(From "Wonders of the Past")

Subtle proof is found in the literal translation of "The Nimrûd Inscription of Tiglath-pileser III," by S. A. Strong. It speaks of tribute received from "the chiefs of the cities of the mountains," consisting of "horses, mules, humped <u>oxen</u>, <u>oxen</u>, and sheep." Sayce says this repetition is "plainly to be traced in the original" — British Museum piece K3751. After speaking of an elaborate entrance-hall that he built for a god, his "majesty in Calah," — "after the fashion of a palace of the Hittites"; in the inverted word-order of ancient Assyrian, the King says: "Lions, <u>bulls</u>, (winged) <u>bulls</u>, formed with exceeding cunning, <u>skillfully fashioned</u>, the entrances I caused to hold, and for wonderment I set up." Strong inserted the word "winged," and probably added "humped." These repetitions are not mistakes — not in a Royal Proclamation! They probably denote two slightly different animals of the same breed. One happens to be born with two horns; the other, with one — a unicorn!

A SYMBOL OF CHRIST BY HIS SACRED TREE OF ETERNAL LIFE
(On Esarhaddon's Basalt Stela — Brit. Museum — #91027)

Above we see a priest standing before an altar that
embraces The Sacred Tree of Eternal Life. The great number of horns symbolize the Father, and the rising flames
exemplify the Holy Spirit emanating from the Godhead.
"The Father is in me," says Christ, "and I am in him,"
and the "gods, unto whom the word of God came," knew Him,
and they knew the Godhead (Romans 1: 20-32). It was their
responsibility to teach the sons of men about God. But
since the precious holy Ghost had not yet come, the sons
of men were unable to feel His presence. They walked by
sight, and not by faith. Therefore, the gods had to teach
them by sight. Huge monuments were built, and modeled
after the powerful, but familiar, creatures that freely
roamed the earth, like the terrifying lion, the powerful
bull, the deadly eagle, the mighty unicorn, and even the
miraculous gods themselves. Wings were sometimes added
to express the lofty nature of the heavenly beings, and
finally the sons of men began to believe in God because
they saw the likenesses of His powers that ruled the
heavens and the earth. These impressive monuments were
the sacred and beloved genies or cherubim of the Assyrians, the Babylonians, the Persians — and yes, even the
Hebrews; and serious problems arose when the people began to worship these inanimate memorials instead of what
they represented. Jehovah, the Lord God of Israel, re-
buked Israel for this, but they still persisted in their
idolatry; and the Bible certainly verifies all of this.

AN ASSYRIAN WINGED BULL OR CHERUB
(Perrot and Chipiez)

The following excerpts from "The Popular and Critical
Bible Encyclopaedia and Scriptural Dictionary" give us
some interesting details on the very high value that the
Israelites placed upon these cherubim:

> Figures of the cherubim were conspicuous implements
> in the Levitical tabernacle. Two of them were placed
> at each end of the mercy-seat, standing in a stooping
> attitude, as if looking down towards it, while they
> overshadowed it with their expanded wings, and, in-
> deed, they were component parts of it, formed out of
> the same mass of pure gold as the mercy-seat itself
> (Exod. xxv:19).
>
> These figures were afterwards transferred to the
> most holy place in Solomon's temple, and it has been
> supposed from 1 Chron. xxviii:18 that that prince
> constructed two additional ones after the same pat-

tern, and of the same solid and costly material, but whether it was with a view to increase their number in accordance with the more spacious and magnificent edifice to which they were removed, or merely to supply the place of those made by Moses, which in the many vicissitudes that befell the ark might have been mutilated or entirely separated from the mercy-seat to which they were attached — is not ascertained. This much, however, is known, that Solomon erected two of colossal dimensions in an erect posture with their faces towards the walls (2 Chron. iii: 13), covering with their outstretched wings the entire breadth of the debir, or most holy place. These sacred hieroglyphics were profusely embroidered on the tapestry of the tabernacle, on the curtains and the great veil that separated the holy from the most holy place (Exod. xxvi:1-31), as well as carved in several places (1 Kings viii:6-8) on the walls, doors and sacred utensils of the temple.

The position occupied by these singular images at each extremity of the mercy-seat — while the Shechinah or sacred flame that symbolized the Divine presence and the awful name of Jehovah in written characters were in the intervening space — gave rise to the well-known phraseology of the sacred writers, which represents the Deity dwelling between or inhabiting the cherubim, and, in fact, so intimately associated were they with the manifestation of the Divine glory that whether the Lord is described as at rest or in motion, as seated on a throne, or riding in a triumphal chariot, these symbolic figures were essential elements in the description (Num. vii:89; Ps. xviii: 10; lxxxx: i; xcix:1-10; Is. vi:2; xxxvii:16).

The symbolic religious figures of their neighbors may have had a more profound effect upon the minds of the Hebrew prophets than is commonly acknowledged. These awe-inspiring cherubim constantly overshadowed the daily chores of the captive prophets and their people. They eventually would have had some impact on their conception of the divine powers above, as Dr. Layard indicates when he says:

AN ORNAMENT FROM THE N. W. PALACE OF NIMRUD
(From Layard's "Nineveh and Its Remains")

The resemblance between the symbolic figures I have
described, and those seen by Ezekiel in his vision,
can scarcely fail to strike the reader. As the prophet had beheld the Assyrian palaces, with their mysterious images and gorgeous decorations, it is highly
probable that, when seeking to typify certain divine attributes, and to describe the divine glory, he
chose forms that were not only familiar to him, but
to the people whom he addressed — captives like himself in the land of Assyria. Those who were uncor-
rupted by even the outward forms of idolatry, sought
for images to convey the idea of the Supreme God.
Ezekiel saw in his vision the likeness of four living
creatures, which had four faces, four wings, and the
hands of a man under their wings on their four sides.
Their faces were those of a man, a lion, an ox, and an
eagle. By them was a wheel, the appearance of which
"was as it were a wheel in the middle of a wheel." It
will be observed that the four forms chosen by Ezekiel to illustrate his description — the man, the lion,
the bull, and the eagle, — are precisely those which
are constantly found on Assyrian monuments as religious types. The "wheel within a wheel," mentioned
in connection with the emblematical figures, may refer to the winged circle, or wheel, representing at
Nimroud the supreme deity. These coincidences are
too marked not to deserve notice; and do certainly
lead to the inference, that the symbols chosen by the
prophet were derived from the Assyrian sculptures.

AN ORNAMENT FROM THE N. W. PALACE OF NIMRUD
(From Layard's "Nineveh and Its Remains")

Apparently after the Flood the descendants of Adam, "the son of God" (Luke 3:38), such as Asshur — a distant son of God, who undoubtedly received a lot of antediluvian common knowledge, divine histories, and prophecies (i.e. Gen. 3:15) from his forefathers, had brought the Word to his people; and the reverence of divine symbols carried over into the late Assyrian empire. Dr. Layard has just a little more to say about these symbolic cherubim he found so frequently in Assyrian ornamentation:

> That the Assyrians possessed a highly refined taste can hardly be questioned, when we find them inventing an ornament which the Greeks afterwards, with few additions and improvements, so generally adopted in their most classic monuments. Others, no less beautiful, continually occur in the most ancient basreliefs of Nimroud. The sacred bull, with expanded wings, and the wild goat, are introduced kneeling before the mystic flower . . . . The same animals are occasionally represented supporting disks, or flowers and rosettes. A bird, or human figure, frequently takes the place of the bull and goat; and the simple flower becomes a tree, bearing many flowers of the same shape. This tree, evidently a sacred symbol, is elaborately and tastefully formed; and is one of the most conspicuous ornaments of Assyrian sculpture.

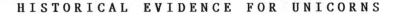

PAINTED BRICKS THAT BRIGHTENED AN ASSYRIAN PALACE
(From Layard's "Monuments of Nineveh" — From Nimrûd)

The illustrations of Assyrian ornamentations shown above and on the following page are good examples of the type Layard found at Nimrûd. On the painted bricks to the left, yellow and blue are the favorite colors of the Assyrian artists. The wingless unicorns are probably representative of the type commonly found running in the wilds. In the fruitful pattern sewn on the king's robe, we see winged gods sustaining their eternal existence by plucking the fruit of the Sacred Tree of Eternal Life. This reminds us of "the tree of life," spoken of in the Book of Genesis, and the one spoken of in the 22nd chapter of Revelation which, like the Assyrian tree, sprouts several types of fruit. The gods are the lower ranking

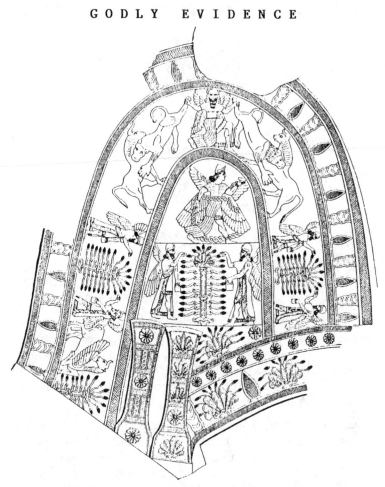

SYMBOLIC EMBROIDERIES ON THE KING'S ROBE
(From Layard's "Monuments of Nineveh")

sort because they bear only two horns. The top god is
pulling back the lions springing for the jugulars of the
unicorns — like the devil "seeking whom he may devour."
    That the Assyrian tree of life bore different flowers
or fruit at different times — like the one in the Book of
Revelation — is confirmed by Dr. Layard when he says:

> The flowers at the ends of the branches are fre-
> quently replaced in later Assyrian monuments, and on
> cylinders, by the fir or pine cone, and sometimes by a
> fruit or ornament resembling the pomegranate. . . .

THE ASSYRIAN TREE OF LIFE AFTER THE POMEGRANATE
(From Layard——N. W. Palace, Nimrûd)

Such perhaps was "the net-work with pomegranates,"
one of the principal ornaments in the temple of Solomon. (1 Kings, vii. 41, 42.) The pomegranate was
worked on the garments of Aaron, (Exodus xxvii. 33,
34.) It was evidently a sacred symbol, and was connected with the god Rimmon.

"Rimmon" is a curious word. Many Bible-scholars dis-
agree on the meaning of this important word found several times in the Scriptures. It was "a deity worshipped
by the Syrians of Damascus, where there was a temple or
house of Rimmon (2 K. V. 18). Serarius refers the name
to the Heb. 'rimmon,' a pomegranate, a fruit sacred to
Venus, who is thus the deity worshipped under this title," states Smith's Dictionary of the Bible. Let's remember that Christ said "I am the root and the offspring
of David, and the bright and morning star," (Rev. 22:16)
——which is Venus. Besides the seven-leaf flower resem-
bling the pomegranate, another fruit found on the Sacred
Tree was the pine cone. Layard says: "M. Lajard, in an
elaborate essay, has shown the connection between the
cone of the cypress, and the worship of Venus in the religious systems of the East." From the lofty mountains
of Ararat the Word streamed down with the Hurrians and

Sumerians to Mesopotamia, and the priests there became
adept astronomers who maintained a thorough Scriptural
record of the origin of our planetary system——much more
detailed than Genesis——and Venus is comparable therein
to the Lamb that was slain from the foundation of the
world——Jesus. That foundation was laid during a cruel
episode of planetary violence long ago. Also, the Bible
speaks of Rimmon as a particular rock, and that is not
difficult to associate with Jesus, "the very rock of our
salvation," as the Christians would say. Furthermore,
another curious note is that the LORD of Israel publicly
healed Naaman of leprosy. He was a worshiper who bowed
himself "in the house of Rimmon." After his healing,
Elisha, the man of God, told him to go in peace. Would
he say this to an Assyrian idolater? Would the LORD publicly heal a foreign idolater? This indicates that both
Elisha and his God, at least, tacitly approved of the
bowing before Rimmon (II Kings, Chap. 5) because they
probably knew he was not an idolater at all, as some
theologians suggest, but a true worshiper of the coming
Savior——symbolized by Rimmon, the one-horned bull ox,
or Unicorn. Smith's Dictionary also says that Seldon
proposes "that Rimmon is from the root 'rûm,' 'to be
high' and signifies 'most high,' like the Phoenician
'Elioun,' and Heb. 'elyôn.'" Yet, most Bible-dictio-
naries simply define Rimmon as only the pomegranate,
from its "upright" growth; but the Hebrew word "rîm,"
translated as "unicorn," in the King James Authorized
Translation of the Bible, is also derived from a Hebrew
root word of a similar meaning—— to "be lifted up"——
so there is a very close symbolic connection between
the Pomegranate, Rimmon, Venus, the Unicorn, and Jesus.

In her work titled "The Unicorn Tapestries," Margaret
B. Freeman offers some interesting interpretations of
the symbolic pomegranate:

> The pomegranate, says Hrabanus Maurus, "under the
> circle of the rind contains a multitude of seeds.
> The pomegranate is the Church or the unity of faith
> and the concord of peace." He explains that even as
> the pomegranate has many seeds under one rind, so the
> Church has assembled in it many people of different

POMEGRANATES.

sorts and yet has grace. The pomegranate is also a symbol of the plenitude and hope, for "the Israelite explorers who were sent into the Promised Land brought back pomegranates with grapes and figs, as is told in the Book of Numbers." Hrabanus quotes further the verse in the Song of Songs (Vulgate 6:6) where the bride says to the bridegroom, "Thy cheeks are as the bark of a pomegranate, besides what is hidden within thee." And thus, with the church, these things "that are seen are exceedingly great, but much greater are those that are not seen and are reserved for the future." Here, then, it is implied that the pomegranate is a symbol of an afterlife and a promise of immortality.

According to Cassiodorus and Bede, the pomegranate also may signify Christ. Just as "one must open (the pomegranate) and look into the interior, where such precious fragrant juice and scent flows forth, so must one also penetrate into the inner suffering of the Redeemer, in order to contemplate the boundless soul-suffering of the heart of God whose blood flows over all mankind."

The ancient Chaldean engraving above seems to show Eve after the Fall. The Devil snaking up behind the woman seems to be listening and whispering in her ear while she pleads her case with the horned god on the right. In his "Story of Chaldea," Zénaïde Ragozin, says:

The remarkable cylinder with the human couple and the serpent leads us to the consideration of a most important object in the ancient Babylonian or Chal-

A DIVINE LECTURE IN THE GARDEN OF EDEN
(From George Smith's "Chaldean Genesis")

dean religion—the Sacred Tree, the Tree of Life. .
. . which remains invariable both in such Babylonian
works of art as we possess and on the Assyrian sculptures, where the tree, or a portion of it appears not
only in the running ornaments on the walls but on seal
cylinders and even in the embroidery on the robes of
kings. In the latter case indeed, it is almost certain, from the belief in talismans which the Assyrians had inherited, along with the whole of their
religion from the Chaldean mother country, that this
ornament was selected not only as appropriate to the
sacredness of the royal person, but as a consecration
and protection. The holiness of the symbol is further evidenced by the kneeling posture of the animals which sometimes accompany it (see Fig. 222, page
67), --(shows a unicorn)-- and the attitude of adoration of the human figures, or winged spirits attend-
ing it, by the prevalence of the sacred number seven
in its component parts, and by the fact that it is
reproduced on a great many of those glazed earthenware coffins which are so plentiful at Warka (ancient
Erech). This latter fact clearly shows that the tree-
symbol not only meant life in general, life on earth,
but a hope of life eternal, beyond the grave, or why
should it have been given to the dead? These coffins
at Warka belong, it is true, to a late period, some as
late as a couple of hundred years after Christ, but
the ancient traditions and their meaning had, beyond
a doubt, been preserved. Another significant detail
is that the cone is frequently seen in the hands of
men or spirits, and always in a way connected with
worship or auspicious protection; sometimes it is

THE ASSYRIAN TRINITY TREE OF ETERNAL LIFE
(Perrot and Chipiez)

held to the king's nostrils by his attendant protect-
ing spirits, (known by their wings); a gesture of unmistakable significancy, since in ancient languages
"the breath of the nostrils" is synonymous with "the
breath of life."

The sacred tree to the left bears an obvious array of numerical patterns. A fleur-de-lis or cross — a noted sign of the Savior — crowns the god's head and supports the tree. Up from the divine root run three arteries that spirit life-giving blood to fruit on the branches. The root or cross also nurtures the four low sprouts that bear twelve seeds — the twelve tribes of Israel spreading the Word to the world. Three bands secure the god's crown and embrace his wrists and strong upper right arm. The three points on the three spheres hanging on three thongs may symbolize certain elements of the Trinity.

Seven is the Lord God's number, and 7 sets of divine seed on the higher branches go to heaven, meaning living victory, and 2 X 7 fall to earth, spelling deadly defeat.

Five is the number of the angels or gods. Ten branches fall on the tree, denoting the fallen godly branches of the eternal tree of life, which sprang from the ten great antediluvian kings. One third (21) are rising to heaven while two thirds (42) are pointed toward hell. The four-horned god (Zech. 1:18) holds the powerful triple triad with the five digits of his lowered left hand and points to heaven with the five of his raised right hand.

Five is also the number of Grace, represented by the five letters in JESUS, and in his "Number in Scripture," E. W. Bullinger has a little more to say about this:

> "Five" is four "plus" one (4 + 1). We have had hitherto the three persons of the Godhead, and their manifestation in creation. Now we have a further revelation of a People called out from mankind, redeemed and saved, to walk with God from earth to heaven. Hence, Redemption follows creation. Inasmuch as in consequence of the fall of man creation came under the curse and was "made subject to vanity," therefore man and creation must be redeemed. Thus we have: 1. Father. 2. Son. 3. Spirit 4. Creation 5. Redemption.
> These are the five great mysteries, and five is therefore the number of GRACE.

In place of the three spheres carried by the god in the previous illustration, Assyrian divinities sometimes were portrayed before the Sacred Tree of Eternal Life

ASSYRIAN SYMBOLS OF THE HOLY GHOST
(From Layard and Rawlinson)

with an elaborately decorated basket with doves woven beneath the handle like those above. In other places "the figure commonly bears in the right hand either a pomegranate or a pine-cone," says Rawlinson, "while the left is either free or else supports a sort of plaited bag or basket." He adds that "it is an object of great elegance, always elaborately and sometimes very tastefully ornamented. Possibly it may represent the receptacle in which the divine gifts are stored." Elsewhere a huge dove is lugged along on the shoulders of four men. Among Christians of the early Church (called-out ones), the dove was the symbol reserved especially for the holy Ghost; and the special numerical value associated with Him is FIFTY — like that at the bottom of this page.

In the 16th printing of Evangelist Ed. F. Vallowe's "Biblical Mathematics," he says: "Fifty is the number connected with the Holy Spirit and His work. The Holy Spirit was poured out on the day of Pentecost, which was FIFTY days after the resurrection of Christ." Actually, the original 1611 King James Bible uses "holy Ghost" instead of "Holy Spirit," but Vallowe may be a victim of the thousands of revisions that the original Bible has had to endure over the centuries. In the New Testament, 1 John 5:7-8 show that the "holy Ghost" and "the Spirit" are two different entities.

"Holy Spirit" is mentioned seven times in the Bible, three times in the Old Testament, once by Christ in the New, followed by three other instances. When Jesus links up these two trios in Luke 11:13, He refers to that Gift being given, upon request, by "your" heavenly Father; so the holy Spirit is joined to the Father. The holy Ghost, used only in the New Testament, is linked to the Son.

According to the archaeological evidence discovered in the ruins of Assyria, the ancients, like Christians today, believed in a Trinity, with a supreme God at its head. George Rawlinson confirmed the fact that the Assyrians had worshiped a supreme God when he wrote:

> At the head of the Assyrian Pantheon stood the "great god," Asshur. His usual titles are "the great Lord," "the King of all the Gods," "he who rules supreme over the Gods." Sometimes he is called "the Father of the Gods," . . . . His place is always first in invocations. He is regarded throughout all the Assyrian inscriptions as the special tutelary deity both of the kings and of the country. He places the monarchs upon their throne, firmly establishes them in the government, lengthens the years of their reigns, preserves their power, protects their forts and armies, makes their name celebrated, and the like. To him they look to give them victory over their enemies, to grant them all the wishes of their heart, and to allow them to be succeeded on their thrones by their sons, and their sons' sons, to a remote posterity. Their usual phrase when speaking of him is "Asshur, my Lord." They represent themselves as passing their lives in his service. It is to spread his worship that they carry on their wars. They fight, ravage, destroy in his name. Finally, when they subdue a country, they are careful to "set up the emblems of Asshur," and teach the people his laws and his worship.

> The tutelage of Asshur over Assyria is strongly marked by the identity of his name with that of the country, which in the original is complete. It is also indicated by the curious fact that, unlike the other gods, Asshur had no notorious temple or shrine in any particular city of Assyria, a sign that his

THE TRINITY SYMBOL OF ASSHUR
(From the Signet Cylinder of King Sennacherib)

worship was spread equally throughout the whole land, and not to any extent localized. As the national deity, he had indeed given name to the original capital; but even at Asshur ("Kileh-Sherghat") it may be doubted whether there was any building which was specially his. Under these circumstances it is a reasonable conjecture that all the shrines throughout Assyria were open to his worship, to whatever minor god they might happen to be dedicated.

In the inscriptions the Assyrians are constantly described as "the servants of Asshur," and their enemies as "the enemies of Asshur." The Assyrian religion is "the worship of Asshur." No similar phrases are used with respect to any of the other gods of the Pantheon.

The Assyrians probably named their supreme God after one of their ancient forefathers, Asshur, a son of Shem and the grandson of Noah. He had powers attributed to him like those the Hebrews recognized in Jehovah.

But the Lord of Israel's were apparently greater. He seems to have had the ability to destroy Nineveh, and it seems Asshur could do little to prevent it. But the LORD kindly sent His reluctant prophet Jonah up there to warn the city, or the people and their "God" or gods (Elohim) to repent from their evil. If we understand "God" to be singular and synonymous with the LORD in the biblical account, then Jehovah must have repented himself! And if so, and it is believed the LORD Jehovah is the omniscient and universal Father, then He has a serious flaw! and some may be worshiping a less-than-perfect Entity.

"And the word of the LORD came unto Jonah the second time," (Jon. 3:1); so Jonah finally obeyed and accomplished the mission he was sent on by the LORD (Jehovah). The royal decree said let man and beast "cry mightily unto God" (Elohim—the gods): and let them turn every one from the violence that is in their hands (Jon. 3:8).

"And <u>God</u>" (the gods) "saw <u>their</u> works, that <u>they</u> turned from <u>their evil way</u>; and <u>God</u>" (the gods) "repented of the <u>evil</u> that he" (Jehovah) "had said that he" (Jehovah) "would do unto <u>them</u>; and he" (Jehovah) "did it not." (Jon. 3:10). Because translators of the Old Testament rendered the plural Hebrew word "Elohim" into the singular English word "God" around 2000 times, and since only 200 or so times did they render that word into English as "gods," many Bible-readers think that God (the gods) and the Lord (Jehovah) are the same. That is one of the furthest things from the truth! Technically though, since the created gods were sent as angels or messengers to earth by God the Father, then the Hebrew word for "gods" that was translated as "God" into English could rightly be comprehended as one God since the gods were, in essence, of their singular creator, God the Father. But by the Bible-translators not making a consistent distinction of number in English — as there still is in Hebrew, it has generated a tremendous amount of confusion and misunderstanding in the minds of English Bible-readers. And the statements made by such learned men as Zénaïde A. Ragozin only barely tip off the readers that something is really amiss. And even he, in his "Story of Chaldea," only hints at the scope of the polytheism (the belief in many gods) that thrived among the Sumerians, Chaldeans, Assyrians, Persians, and yes, even among the Hebrews; but at least, Ragozin has courage to admit:

> In one or two passages, indeed, we do find an expression which seems to have slipped in unawares, as an involuntary reminiscence of an original polytheism; it is where God, communing with himself on Adam's trespass, says: "Behold, the man is become <u>as one of us</u>, to know good and evil" (Gen. 3:22). An even clearer trace confronts us in one of the two names that are given to God. These names are "Jehovah," (more correctly "Yahveh") and "Elohim." Now the latter name is the plural of 'El,' "god," and so really means "the gods." If the sacred writers retained it, it was certainly not from carelessness or inadvertence. As they use it, it becomes in itself almost a profession of faith.

SERVING THE ENTHRONED GOD "EL"
(A Stone Monument from Ras Shamra)

When he mentions God communing with himself, it was not with the Trinity, as he might be implying. Neither Christ nor the holy Ghost had yet come. The Bible says it was the "Lord God," or Chief of the gods. He was talking to some of the lower gods. Genesis says God (the gods or Elohim) created the heaven and earth, and so does the Chaldean account. But, they did it through the power, wisdom, and discretion of the LORD, who indirectly affirmed it when He told Jeremiah (10:11) to tell the house of Israel: "Thus shall ye say unto them, The gods that have not made the heavens and the earth, even they shall parish from the earth, and from under these heavens." They were also corrupted by the flesh, sinned, and even taught men evil; so they too would have to die like men. The Bible and the Book of Enoch bear this out thoroughly.

Above is a photograph of a man serving a drink to the elderly god "El" (the Hebrew singular of "Elohim"). This thirteenth-century memorial was found in Palestine. He is identified with the word "Tor" (meaning "Bull").

THE SEMITIC GOD BAAL
(Another Stone Memorial from Ras Shamra)

"Of the multitudinous divinities of the ancient East," says E. Royston Pike, "perhaps the best known is the one who in our Scriptures is denominated Baal, the god whom the children of Israel preferred time and time again to Jahveh, for whom Ahab reared an altar; the god whose priests, egged on by Elijah's mockings, leaped up and down, slashed themselves with knives and lancets, from morning even until noon; the god for whom the chosen youth of Judah's kingdom passed through the fires of sacrifice."

Above are our drawings of a fragmented artifact of a Hurrian god, Tesheba, riding on The Divine Promise, the Unicorn; and of a seal with a bull, unicorn, and crosses that the ancient Minoans are believed to have worshiped. The memorials show the gods revered bulls, unicorns, and crosses. All relate to the coming Christ. A double cross means a double Savior, twice over, once for god, once for man, both born from the bull-headed Father. Two-horned Tesheba is shown riding home on the back of his Savior!

The early Assyrian artwork reproduced on the next page brings to mind the famous Unicorn Hunt woven into the beautiful medieval European tapestries so aptly written about in Margaret Freeman's beautiful book. It reports:

> On permanent exhibition at The Cloisters, in New York, seven late Gothic tapestries portray the Hunt of the unicorn. Like the unicorn himself, they are one of the marvels of the world, for in no other work of art anywhere is the pursuit and capture of the magical creature presented in such astonishing detail, with such command of pictorial verisimilitude and symbolic intention.
>
> In a duality not rare in the late Middle Ages, the imagery is both secular and religious. The reference to love, matrimonial fidelity, and desire for progeny are understandable in an ensemble that may have celebrated a marriage. But the unicorn, at the same time, is Christ, and the compositions reflect the Incarnation, the Passion, and the Resurrection.

Split hooves are marked features on Assyrian unicorns. Besides the many bas-reliefs and other ornamentations

AN EARLY ASSYRIAN UNICORN HUNT
(From Rawlinson's "Five Great Monarchies")

that emphasize this trait; even the colossal winged bull
in the British museum clearly exhibits split hooves on
every foot. And a split-hoofed unicorn is clearly portrayed in the previous sacrificial scene; so the marked
emphasis placed on this feature is surely significant.
And the idea of using this particular type of animal for
offerings may have influenced the sacrificial laws, for
clean animals, with split hooves, that the neighboring
Hebrews observed. In his work titled "Sacred Geography
and Antiquities," Dr. E. P. Barrows points out the close
relationship shown in the Scriptures between the clean
animals of the ox-type and the unicorns, which thereby
infers that they were the same kind. He explains that:

> When other animals are associated with the unicorn,
> they are always "of the ox kind." Thus in Deut. 33:17,
> the "bullock" and "unicorn" are named together; in
> Ps. 29:6, the "calf" and "young unicorn": in Isa. 34:
> 6, 7, all the clean animals in use for sacrifices are
> named, and with them unicorns — in ver. 6, the small
> cattle, lambs, goats, rams; in verse 7, the large
> cattle, "unicorns, bullock, bulls": in the twenty-
> second Psalm the sufferer describes his enemies as
> "bulls" of Bashan, roaring "lions," and "dogs" (Ver.
> 12, 13, 16); and he prays for deliverance from them in
> the inverse order, as "dogs," "lions," and unicorns"
> (vers. 20, 21). See also the description of the uni-
> corn in Job 39:9-12, from which passage we learn that
> the unicorn "had not yet been tamed."

AN EARLY ASSYRIAN KING HUNTING UNICORNS
(From Rawlinson's "Five Great Monarchies")

Once more: it is obvious that the unicorn is not a foreign animal known to the Hebrews by report only, but one which they "knew from observation."

We come then with much certainty to the conclusion that the unicorn was a "wild animal of the ox kind."

Above we have an illustration of a royal unicorn hunt drawn from one of the earlier Assyrian ornamentations. George Rawlinson discusses the ancient Assyrian animal life at various points in his several volumes comprising "The Five Great Monarchies." From this work we have extracted and loosely combined some of his rare knowledge of Assyrian unicorn hunts, and we recite it as follows:

> The Assyrian monarchs chased the wild bull in their chariots without dogs, but with the assistance of horsemen, who turned the animals when they fled, and brought them within the monarch's reach. The king then aimed his arrows at them, and the attendant horsemen, who were provided with bows, seem to have been permitted to do the same. The bull seldom fell until he had received a number of wounds; and we sometimes see as many as five arrows still fixed in the body of one that has succumbed.

> The pursuit of the wild bull is represented with more frequency and in greater detail upon the early sculptures than even that of the lion. In the Nimrud series we see the bull pursued by chariots, horsemen, and footmen, both separately and together. We observe him prancing among reeds, reposing, fighting with

the lion, charging the king's chariot, wounded and falling, fallen, and lastly laid out in state for the final religious ceremony. No such elaborate series illustrates the chase of the rival animal.

It seems nearly certain that, in the time of the later kings, the species of wild cattle previously hunted, whatever it was, had disappeared from Assyria altogether; at least this is the only probable account that can be given of its non-occurrence in the later sculptures, more especially in those of Asshur-banipal, the son of Esar-haddon, which seem intended to represent the chase under every aspect known at the time. We might therefore presume it to have been, even in the early period, already a somewhat rare animal. And so we find in the Inscriptions that the animal, or animals, which appear to represent wild cattle, were only met with in outlying districts of the empire — on the borders of Syria and in the country about Harran; and then in such small numbers as to imply that even there they were not very abundant.

There are two animals mentioned in the Tiglath-Pileser Inscription which have been brought to represent wild cattle. . . .

The Assyrian word in the first of the two passages is read as "Rim," and the animal should therefore be identical with the "Rim" (in Hebrew characters) of Holy Scripture. Although the Arabs give the name of "Raim" to a large antelope, and a similar use of that term seems to have been known in Egypt (Layard, "Nineveh and Its Remains," vol. ii. p. 429), yet the Hebrew term "Rim" appears, from a comparison of the passages in which it occurs, almost certainly to mean an animal of the ox kind. (See especially Is. xxxiv. 17, where it is joined with the domestic bull, and Job xxxix. 9-12, where the questions drive their force from an implied comparison with that animal.)

Four "Rims" only are mentioned as slain. Of the other animal ten were slain and four taken. Of lions on the same expedition Tiglath-Pileser slew a hundred and twenty.

THE DEATH OF THE UNICORN
(From Rawlinson)

When the chase of the nobler animals — the lion and the wild bull — had been conducted to a successful issue, the hunters returned in a grand procession to the capital, carrying with them as trophies of their prowess the bodies of the slain. These were borne aloft on the shoulders of men, three or four being required to carry each beast. Having been brought to an appointed spot, they were arranged side by side upon the ground, the heads of all pointing the same way; and the monarch, attended by several of his principal officers, as the Vizier, the chief Eunuch, the fan-bearers, the bow and mace bearers, and also by a number of musicians, came to the place and solemnly poured a libation over the prostrate forms, first however (as it would seem) raising the cup to his own lips. It is probable that this ceremony had to some extent a religious character. The Assyrian monarchs commonly ascribe the success of their hunting expeditions to the gods Nin (or Ninip) and Nergal; and we may well understand that a triumphant return would be accompanied by a thank-offering to the great protectors under whose auspices success had been achieved.

With respect to Muss-Arnolt's translation of "wild oxen," for the Assyrian word found in the Inscription of Tiglath-pileser I — where we injected our rendering of "(unicorns)," quoting an eminent Irish Orientalist, Mr. Rawlinson says: "Dr. Hincks reads the word used as "Rim," which would clearly be identical with the Hebrew translated in our version 'unicorn.'"

CHAPTER THREE

MORE EVIDENCE

In the reign of Tiglath-pileser I, eleven centuries before Christ, Assyria was engaged in an active campaign to expand her frontiers in the north-west; but she apparently overtaxed her strength, for after the death of that king, her power began to decline, and she suffered heavy defeats thereafter.

But at the beginning of the ninth century, she began to recuperate and initiated a campaign to recover her former glory. Under Tukulti-Adar II, Babyloinia was subdued; and he passed on his enlarger and more prosperous kingdom to his son Assur-nasir-pal about 885 B.C. From that time on Assyria pursued a ruthless but successful policy of expanding her boundaries at the expense of her neighbors. The king set an unforgettable example for his successors. He had his opponents cruelly flayed and impaled, and then boasted of his monstrous victories on the permanent monuments of stone which adorned his new capital at Calah (modern Nimrûd) that he built forty miles north of his old seat of government at Ashur. His new palace was embellished with the typical Assyrian style of artwork — bas-reliefs portraying the favorite royal sports, lion and unicorn hunting, along with more extensive pictorial and written commemorations of the ravaging and plundering campaigns that led to Assyrian domination in all directions. Under his rule, Assyria became the greatest and most vicious fighting machine the ancient world had yet seen or felt.

And the fierce conquests of his notorious son Shalmaneser (circa 860-825 B.C.) even surpassed those of his father. He even succeeded in crushing and subjugating

THE BLACK OBELISK FROM NIMRUD
(From Layard — after Birch)

the Syrians of Damascus in 842 B.C. Then, out of fear of suffering the same fate, the smaller nearby nations hastened to pay tribute to the undisputed conqueror who utterly squashed their once powerful neighbor. There is no evidence that even King Jehu resisted in turning Israel over as a vassal state to Assyria. He too paid tribute to its victorious oppressor. This is verified by the record engraved on the famous "Black Obelisk" which Shalmaneser set up at his palace at Nimrûd.

In describing the ancient Assyrian monuments dug up in the last century, Orientalist and Camden professor of ancient history at Oxford, George Rawlinson (brother of English Assyriologist Sir Henry), says the stone obelisks were few and mostly in fragmentary condition, but

JEHU SUBMITTING TO ASSYRIAN KING SHALMANESER
(From the Black Obelisk—British Museum Piece No. 98)

One alone is perfect—the obelisk in black basalt,
discovered by Mr. Layard at Nimrûd, which has now for
many years been in the British Museum. This monument
is sculptured on each of its four sides, in part with
writing and in part with bas-reliefs. It is about
seven feet high, and two feet broad at the base, tapering gently towards the summit, which is crowned
with three low steps, or gradines. The inscription,
which occupies the upper and lower portion of each
side, and is also carried along the spaces between
the bas-reliefs, consists of 210 clearly cut lines,
and is one of the most important documents that has
come down to us.

There are 190 lines of cuneiform writing on the lower
part of the four sides. It details the principal events
of Shalmaneser's reign and relates that the king conducted thirty-one expeditions against the peoples of
various countries. His rule eventually extended south
through Babylonia to the Persian Gulf in the south-east,
to Media in the east, up to Cilicia in the north-west,
and also over to the Mediterranean shores in the west.
The text records two wars against Hazael of Damascus in
the eighteenth and twenty-first years of his reign, and
boasts of the payment of tribute of silver, gold, etc. by

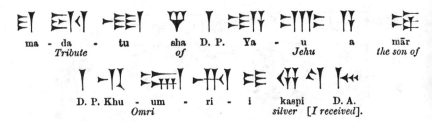

A RENDERING OF THE CUNEIFORM WRITING ABOVE JEHU
(From the work of E. M. Thompson & E. A. W. Budge)

Jehu, which closely corroborates the information given to us in the Bible.

In the transliteration and translation above, "D.P." stands for "Determinative Prefix," and "D. A.," means "Determinative Affix." Dr. Harper reads the whole cuneiform account of Jehu as: "I have received the tribute of Jehu, the son of Omri: silver, gold, bowls of gold, chalices of gold, cups of gold, buckets of gold, lead, a sceptre of the hand of the king (and) spear-shafts (?)."

The discovery of the ancient monument, in which the cuneiform above was inscribed nearly 3000 years ago, is recounted by Dr. Layard in the following words:

> I found the obelisk completely exposed to view. I descended eagerly into the trench, and was immediately struck by the singular appearance, and evident antiquity, of the remarkable monument before me. We raised it from its recumbent position, and, with the aid of ropes, speedily dragged it out of the ruins. Although its shape was that of an obelisk, yet it was flat at the top and cut into three gradines. It was sculptured on the four sides; there were in all twenty small bas-reliefs . . . . The whole was in the best preservation; scarcely a character of the inscription was wanting; and the figures were as sharp and well defined as if they had been carved but a few days before. The king is twice represented, followed by his attendants; a prisoner is at his feet, and his vizir and eunuchs are introducing men leading various animals, and carrying vases and other objects of tribute on their shoulders, or in their hands.

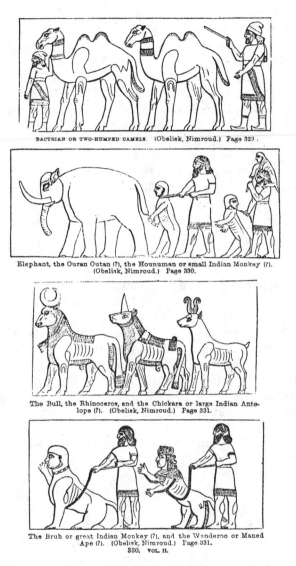

BACTRIAN OR TWO-HUMPED CAMELS. (Obelisk, Nimroud.) Page 329.

Elephant, the Ouran Outan (?), the Hounuman or small Indian Monkey (?).
(Obelisk, Nimroud.) Page 330.

The Bull, the Rhinoceros, and the Chickara or large Indian Antelope (?). (Obelisk, Nimroud.) Page 331.

The Bruh or great Indian Monkey (?), and the Wanderoo or Maned Ape (?). (Obelisk, Nimroud.) Page 331.
330. VOL. II.

DRAWINGS OF BAS-RELIEFS ON THE BLACK OBELISK
(From Layard's "Nineveh and Its Remains")

The animals are the elephant, the rhinoceros, the Bactrian, or two humped camel, the wild bull, the lion, a stag, and various kinds of monkeys.

HISTORICAL EVIDENCE FOR UNICORNS

The illustration on the previous page is a reduced copy of a plate found in A. H. Layard's first American edition of "Nineveh and Its Remains," published in 1849. The central figure in the third relief down from the top is obviously a unicorn. Of all the archaeological works we have studied that contain representations of the bas-reliefs on the Black Obelisk, this is the only one that clearly portrays the unicorn. It seems quite obvious to us that many writers do not want to propagate the idea that the unicorn actually existed. All of the animals displayed on the obelisk are realistic portrayals — except for the monkeys and ape. One can easily sympathize with the lack of Assyrian artistic ability in this area, way back in the primitive ninth century B.C., if one realizes that the Dutch artist Erhard Reuwich (whom we'll meet in a later chapter) had an equally difficult time in accurately portraying the monkey, or ape, in the enlightened fifteenth century A.D. — even with the advantage of 2300 years of artistic experience to rely on.

It is likely Layard's identification of the monkeys and ape is correct, but he is mistaken in labeling the one-horned creature as a rhinoceros. Since he was neither a naturalist nor a translator, he probably would not have recognized a word like "rîmu," which would have identified the creature on the obelisk as the biblical unicorn. And the Irish Orientalist Dr. Edward Hinck's translation of the text, published in the "Dublin University Magazine," didn't come out till October of 1853; so Layard probably would not have known what the Assyrians called the creature until well after his book was published. We strongly suspect that just such a word, like "rîmu," was in the text, and it did tag this prominently displayed animal as the unicorn, even though we do not have a cuneiform transliteration on hand to verify our suspicion. And, in speaking of the "rim" (rîmu) or biblical unicorn, "The Illustrated Bible Dictionary" says: "The word thus rendered has been found in an Assyrian inscription written over the wild ox." We know of no other Assyrian monuments, other than the obelisk, that has this feature; so Layard's unicorn was likely a one-horned bull (male) type of wild ox — not a rhinoceros!

MORE EVIDENCE

The evidence against the rhinoceroses being the "rim" or unicorn of the Bible is considerable. Yet, the Indian variety is, in fact, a real unicorn — a type still alive today. Unlike its two-horned African cousin, it does display only one horn, but that's about the only feature which makes him resemble, even slightly, the unicorn found on the obelisk, or similar animals found on other Assyrian monuments. The Indian variety is enormous, has extremely short legs, wears an entirely different type of coat, sprouts a very unattractive horn, wags a short, flimsy tail, and listens with large, swine-type ears; while the others bear none of these features.

Another reason why the Indian Rhinoceros is not the biblical unicorn is because his feet are terminated by three toes, which are covered with hoof-like nails. The sacrificial animal is required to have split hooves. "Smith's Dictionary of the Bible" says: "Little can be urged in favor of the rhinoceros, for it would have been forbidden to be sacrificed by Moses." And furthermore, in speaking of this biblical "rim" or unicorn, "Calmet's Dictionary of the Holy Bible" states that the arguments held by some that the biblical unicorn ("reem" or "rim") was the rhinoceros

> are however rebutted by the fact that the "reem" was obviously an animal well known to the Hebrews, being every where mentioned with other animals common to the country; while the rhinoceros was never an inhabitant of the country, is no where else spoken of by the sacred writers, nor, according to Bochart, either by Aristotle in his treatise of animals, nor by Arabian writers. Nor do the qualities and habits of the rhinoceros at all coincide with those ascribed to the "reem."

> That the LXX, in using the word "monoceros," (unicorn, one-horn), did not understand by it the rhinoceros, would seem obvious; both because the latter always had its appropriate and peculiar name in Greek (meaning — "rhinoceros, nose-horn"), taken from the position of its horn upon the snout; and also from the circumstance so much insisted on . . . in the extracts

from Mr. Bruce, that the rhinoceros of that part of Africa adjacent to Egypt actually has "two" horns. They appear rather to have had in mind the half-fabulous unicorn, described by Pliny, but lost sight of by all subsequent naturalists; although imperfect hints and accounts of a similar animal have been given by travellers in Africa and India in different centuries, and entirely independent of each other.

The author cited above, who argued in favor of the rhinoceros being the biblical unicorn, is the celebrated Scottish traveller James Bruce. Another celebrity, Dr. John D. Davis, a Professor of Oriental and Old Testament Literature, is convinced that the biblical unicorn was an ox-type of creature, and not an antelope, nor, as some believed, the wild buffalo. He says that the unicorn:

> was possessed of great strength (Numbers xxiii. 22; xxiv. 8), but was too untamable to bend its neck to the yoke, or assist man in his agricultural labors (Job xxxix. 9-12). It was frisky in youth (Ps. xxix. 6). It was not the wild buffalo, for this beast is quite tamable. The R. V. margin (Num. xxiii. 22) renders it by ox-antelope, meaning the oryx ("Antilope leucoryx"). This interpretation is supported by the analogy of the Hebrew "re'em" to the Arabic "rim," which is now used in Syria for the white and yellow gazelle; but the oryx is timid and in ancient Egypt was frequently tamed and used in the plow. There is every reason to believe that the Hebrew word signifies the wild ox (R. V.); for this animal is denoted by the corresponding Assyrian word "rîmu." Admirable representations of it by Assyrian artists show it to be the aurochs ("Bos primigenius"). Tiglathpileser about 1120 to 1100 B. C. hunted it in the land of the Hittites, at the foot of Lebanon. It is now extinct, and its name has been transferred in Syria to another animal; but its previous occurrence on and around Lebanon is independently proved by the fact that Tristram discovered its teeth in the bone caves of Lebanon. Julius Caesar, who met with it in Gaul, described it as the "Bos urus" (Bello Galico vi. 28).

MORE EVIDENCE

After the fierce conquests of the Black-Obelisk King, Shalmaneser III, Assyria's power and dominance in Babylonia began to rise with the succeeding rulers. Under Ashurbanipal (Sardanapalus, 669-626BC) Assyria's glory reached its pinnacle, after he suppressed the urge of its vassal-nations to revolt against Semitic rule.

Elam had conspired to shake loose its Assyrian yoke; so Ashurbanipal made an example of it. He rolled his mighty military machine south, plundered the capital of Susa, and laid bare the rest. He hauled his prisoners and booty to Nineveh and recorded the onslaught in his annals from which the following was translated by John M. P. Smith:

> I destroyed the temple tower of Susa, which was made with an incasement of uknu-stone, and I broke off its turrets, which were made of shining copper. Shushinak, the god of their oracles, who dwells in hidden places, whose divine activity no one sees, Shumudu, Lagámaru, Partikira, Ammankasibar, Uduran, Sapak, whom the kings of Elam worshipped, Husun, Ragiba, Sungursara, Karsa, Kirsamas, Sudanu, Aipaksina, Bilala, Panintimri, Silagara, Napsa, Napirtu, Kindakarpu— these gods and goddesses with their ornaments, their possessions, their furnishings, their priests and temple-servants (?) I carried away to Assyria. I took to Assyria thirty two-statues of kings which were made of silver, gold, copper, and alabaster, from Susa, Madaktu, and Huradi; and also a statue of Ummanigash, son of Umbadara; a statue of Ishtarnanhundi; a statue of Halusi; and a statue of Tammaritu, the second, who had become my servant by the command of Ashur and Ishtar. I threw down the bull-colossi and the guardian gods and all the other watchers of the temple, and I tore down the fierce wild oxen which decorated the doors. I overthrew the temples of Elam until there were no more. . . .
>
> As for Nanna who had been angry for sixteen hundred and thirty-five years and had gone and dwelt in Elam, a place not suitable to her, and who in those days along with the gods, her fathers, had announced my name for lordship over the lands, and had intrusted the return of her divine self to me, saying, "Ashur-

A TEMPLE-HOME OF THE GODS, AND WILD BULLS FROM SUSA
(Right: A Monument from Susa —— Louvre Museum)

banipal shall lead me forth from wicked Elam, and shall cause me to enter E-anna" —— at that time they (i.e. the gods) caused men of later days to see the (execution of) their divine word of command which they had spoken from ancient times. I seized the hand of her great divinity, and with joy of heart she took the straight way to E-anna. On the first day of the month of Kislev I brought her into Erech and gave her a dwelling in E-shargubana, which she loved, in an everlasting shrine.

This last excerpt is important. It adds support to the fact that the gods really existed. Archaeologists have brought to light what pride has stubbornly denied —— and what the Bible has said all along. In the 82nd Psalm GOD makes it perfectly clear: "I have said, Ye are gods; and all of you are children of the most High. But ye shall die like men, and fall like one of the princes," and this is certainly proven by the old relics dug up. No statues of any deities are mentioned; so the aging goddess Nanna must have been held captive alive for those 1635 years.

NANNA PROCEEDING WITH HER FAMILY BACK TO E-ANNA (ERECH)
(From a Relief Found in an Assyrian Palace at Nimrûd)

The informed Dr. Sayce, who said he read "the Babylonian version of the building of the Tower of Babel" on a fragmentary tablet stored in the British Museum, says that the goddess Nanâ (Nanna) "was carried off by the king of Elam, Kudur-nankhundi about 2280 years before Christ." If we subtract 1635 years from the above, we come up with Ashurbanipal taking her by the hand and sending her back home in 645 B.C., the middle of his reign. She certainly lived longer than Adam — if we take the King's word.

And he surely must have known. He ruled over a library of 22,000 religious, literary, and scientific records, including copies of the "olden texts." He proclaims: "The god of scribes has taught me his art. I have learned the secrets of writing. I can even read the intricate tablets in Sumerian; I understand the cryptic words in the stone carvings from the days before the Flood."

Some of these tablets relate to ancient claims that a great celestial war erupted in the primeval past, when the heavenly body that Earth was once part of was split up. The Bible says "They fought from heaven; the stars in their courses fought against Sisera" (Judg. 5:20). NASA's recent photographic probes of our damaged solar system verify the battles were fought. Scientists argue more than ever that the Earth was smashed into and broken up long ago. If the planet is just a remnant of a greater body (Zion), then this may be the clue for the answers to why Venus spins in the opposite direction to other terrestrial planets; why so much war debris drifts along in the asteroid belt where a huge planet probably existed; and why casualties, like our little Moon, greater Venus, and the other neighboring corpses, have lost their life-giving water while the Earth retains so much. The cryptic details that are given in Job, the Psalms, Lamentations, Revelation, and the other prophetic books of the Bible line up very well with the ancient astronomical records. David points to this great battle of the gods, or stars, when he salutes in his Psalms with the word "Selah," which spells "Hales" in reverse. All this urges us to reconsider the first words in the Bible:

> In the beginning
> God created the heaven and the earth.
> And the earth was without form, and void;

When was anything ever created that was void and without form? It seems like a contradiction, but if a christened child is still in the mother's womb, her youngster is seen as "without form, and void" — especially in this present world of abortion — but the child still exists before being born. In the beginning the Earth, as part of mother Zion, was no different. More facts are given in the 66th chapter of Isaiah, the 12th of Revelation, and elsewhere in the Bible. For posterity's sake, the antediluvian priests translated this astronomical data on the origin of the planets into scenes engraved in stone.

Just such a scene is found on a stone tablet of Nabu-pal-iddin, who reigned about 900 BC. It was found carefully preserved in an earthenware coffer in the ruins of the holy city of Sippar, or Sippara, as some spell it. Nearly 300 years after Nabu-pal-iddin, the Chaldean King Nabopolassar, who allied himself with the Medes and helped overthrow and sack Nineveh, found this sacred memorial among the contents of the coffer. He realized it was a copy of an ancient original; so he covered it with a protective coating of clay, in which he described his restoration of the temple that preserved those age-old memories. Nearly 100 years later, during the prophet Daniel's time, in the reign of Nebonidus (556-539 BC), the coffer was opened again, and the relic was given even more protection to preserve its primordial messages.

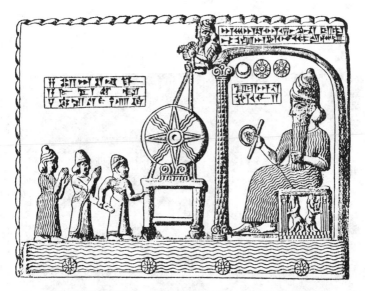

THE HEAVENLY AND EARTHLY WITNESSES
(From the British Museum Piece, No. 12,137)

The scene above, from that sacred relic of Sippar, is thousands of years older than the Bible. The number and placement of the figures remind us of the three heavenly and three earthly witnesses mentioned in 1John 5:7-8. Before the enthroned God rests the Earth on his footstool, and in his hand are a coiled line and a measuring rod that remind us of the questions God asked Job: "Where wast thou when I laid the foundations of the earth? declare, if thou hast understanding. Who hath laid the measures thereof, if thou knowest? or who hath stretched the line upon it? . . . When the morning stars sang together, and all the sons of God shouted for joy?" Those before the throne closely resemble a god, a priest, and a king — all beardless, like the ancient Sumerians who called Sippar "E-Babara." Berossus said their ancient Noah buried the records of the antediluvian world there. Their posterity were certainly astronomically alert for we see four compass-points prominently displayed on a spherical Earth; and its three neighbors, the Moon, Sun, and the EIGHT-pointed planet Venus or "the bright and morning star," all stand high in the background. Number EIGHT in Scriptural Numbers means A NEW BEGINNING — so

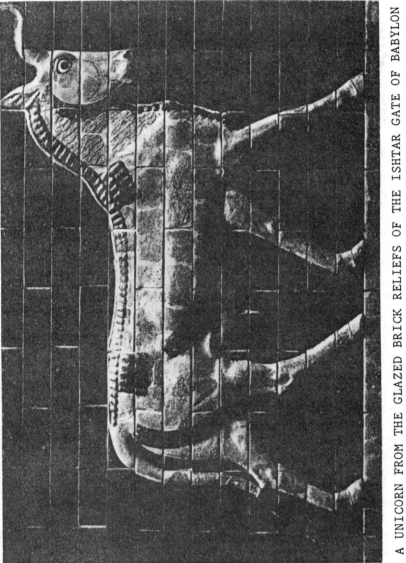

A UNICORN FROM THE GLAZED BRICK RELIEFS OF THE ISHTAR GATE OF BABYLON

Hundreds of lifelike animals like this — each eight feet long — decorated

the Ishtar Gate, according to August Köster of the State Museum Berlin.

UNICORN TRIBUTE & ISHTAR——"THE BRIGHT AND MORNING STAR"
(From Assyrian Memorials Illustrated in Old Text Books)

we worship our Master Jesus on the Eighth Day he arose or
Sonday——as the Scots say! In the Book of Numbers "Moses
told the children of Israel according to all that the
Lord commanded Moses"——"On the Eighth day ye shall have
a solemn assembly: ye shall do no servile work therein."

Ezekiel says there were "EIGHT tables, whereupon they
slew their sacrifices"——of bulls or unicorns——and an
EIGHT-horned God stands above on his winged cherub——a
Unicorn. He dawns an eternal circle with an EIGHT-point
star signifying Venus, the Eighth planet to the Sun. And
Exodus 21:22-25 demands EIGHT clear-cut punishments,
which embody "wound for wound," "stripe for stripe," and
"life for life" (for a mischievous abortion); so a whip,
a bridle, and a rod are seen above in the Master's hands.
They recall a Proverbial saying: "A whip for the horse,
a bridle for the ass, and a rod for the fool's back!"

The Bible repeats 7 (God the Father's number) 8 (the
Son's) times the number EIGHT, and 7 precedes 8 in 78; so
God the Father comes before His promised Son. "Numbers"
says 3 times: ye shall offer on the sixth (man's number),
seventh, and Eighth day "one goat for a sin offering;"
He recalls the unicorn-goat the prophet Daniel spoke of:

> I lifted up mine eyes, and saw, and, behold, there
> stood before the river a ram which had two horns:
> and the two horns were high; but one was higher than
> the other, and the higher came up last. I saw the ram
> pushing westward, and northward, and southward; so
> that no beasts might stand before him, neither was
> there any that could deliver out of his hand; but

he did according to his will, and became great. And as I was considering, behold, an he goat came from the west on the face of the whole earth, and touched not the ground: and the goat had <u>a notable horn</u> between his eyes. And he came to the ram that had two horns, which I had seen standing before the river, and ran unto him in the fury of his power. And I saw him come close unto the ram, and he was moved with choler against him, and smote the ram, and brake his two horns: and there was no power in the ram to stand before him, but he cast him down to the ground, and stamped upon him: and there was none that could deliver the ram out of his hand. Therefore the he goat waxed very great: and when he was strong, <u>the great horn</u> was broken; and for it came up four notable ones toward the four winds of heaven. And out of them came forth a little horn, which waxed exceeding great, toward the south, and toward the east, and toward the pleasant land. . . .

And Daniel sought after the meaning of his vision; so it was explained to the "son of man" in this way:

The ram which thou sawest having two horns are the kings of Media and Persia. And the rough goat is the king of Grecia: and <u>the great horn</u> that is between his eyes is the first king. Now that being broken, whereas four stood up for it, four kingdoms shall stand up out of the nation, but not in his power. And in the latter time of their kingdom, when the transgressors are come to the full, a king of fierce countenance, and understanding dark sentences, shall stand up. And his power shall be mighty, but not by his own power: and he shall destroy wonderfully, and shall prosper, and practise, and shall destroy the mighty and the holy people. . . .

The prophecy was fulfilled. The Lord's "anointed," Cyrus, attacked the drunken, raveling capital city of Babylon, which quickly fell to the Persian army. Shortly thereafter, the rest of Semitic Babylonia succumbed to the new Aryan might; and the Persian Empire expanded rapidly in every direction. (See the map on page 84.)

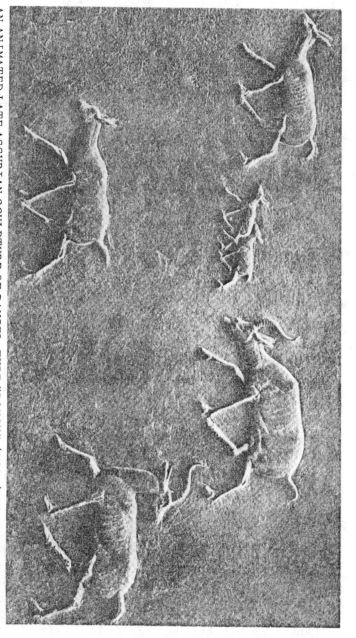

AN ANIMATED LATE ASSYRIAN SCULPTURE OF DANIEL—TYPE "ROUGH" (WILD) GOATS OR UNICORNS
(The work of Ashurbanipal's sculptors——Courtesy of the the British Museum)

Most are grazing very peacefully, unconscious of any danger, but the last seems to wind approaching hunters. Notice the spiraled horns, probably on the male unicorns.

But, a few centuries later, a Greek, or more precisely, a Macedonian rough goat's notable horn broke the horns of the Persian ram, just like Daniel had foretold. And soon after Alexander the Great expired, his empire was sought by "four notable ones," his greedy, jealous generals, or "kings as they were called"—who "fought, quarreled, grasped, and wrangled like loosened tigers in an amphitheater." The decisive battle of "Ipsus" (301 B.C.) determined the outcome. (See the note under the map on page 84.) But later, their dominions were lost to the little Roman horn which waxed exceedingly great. And one of Rome's notorious emperors, with a fierce countenance, "understanding dark sentences," did, in fact, "destroy the mighty and holy people," and, along with them, the Holy City of Jerusalem. (See page 144, in the Appendix.)

In his "Scripture Geography," Thomas T. Smiley, M.D. demonstrated, with a series of four illustrations of ancient symbols, that the identification of the kingdoms in Daniel's prophecy were not only correct, but also, that the number of horns mentioned matched the national emblems of those kingdoms at the time. He says:

> Ancient medals of Persia are yet in existence, which bear the figure of a ram, as the emblem of the Persian nation, and prove that Daniel employed the proper type of Persian dominion, when predicting its overthrow by the single-horned goat of Macedonia. This ram had two horns, "one of which was higher than the other, and the higher came up last." (Dan. viii. 3.) These were the kingdoms of Media and Persia, united under Cyrus, of which the Persian exceeded in power.

And his proof lies with his first "No. 1." illustration on the next page. He describes it as:

> An engraving from an ancient gem representing the appropriate symbols of Persia and Macedonia, under the figures of a ram, and a goat with one horn. This gem was probably engraved in the time of Alexander the Great, and denotes the union of Persia and Macedonia under the same empire. We offer it as affording a remarkable illustration of the emblems employed by Daniel the prophet, to signify those two kingdoms.

MORE EVIDENCE

No. 1.

Dr. Smiley also included a short description of Macedonia in his book, along with his other three numbered
illustrations and descriptions of single-horned goats
symbolizing Daniel's prophecy. We will now set forth the
rest of his material to heighten our burgeoning store-
house of historical evidence for unicorns. In the year
1834, when we still had the freedom to teach the Bible
in our schools, and years before any of the great unicorn
monuments were dug up in the Orient, Smiley explained
— in his Philadelphia publication "INTENDED FOR THE USE
OF FAMILIES AND SCHOOLS" — that Macedonia was

a large province north of Greece; bounded north by
the mountains of Haemus; east by Thracia and the Egean
Sea; south by Thessaly and Epirus, in Greece; and west
by the Ionian and Adriatic seas.

This country was anciently called Aemathia, and has
been supposed by some to have been peopled by the descendants of Madai, the son of Japheth.

Caranus, the first king of Macedonia, began his
reign 814 years before the Christian era. In the
reign of Amyntas I. about 547 years before Christ,
the Macedonians, upon being threatened with inva-
sion, became tributary to the Persians. Having, however, shaken off the Persian yoke, Macedonia continued to increase in power; and at length, during the
reign of Philip, 337 years before Christ, all Greece
was brought under the dominion of this nation. Alexander the Great, son and successor of Philip, raised
Macedonia to its height of power and greatness; and
made it the third kingdom which had obtained the em-

No. 1.

pire of the world, having no less than a hundred and
fifty nations under its dominion. But after the death
of Alexander, the empire, being divided among his
generals, quickly fell into weakness and contention,
and was soon swallowed up in the rising and all conquering power of the Romans. Macedonia, when visited
by the apostle Paul, (Acts xvi.) was a Roman province; and several of its cities, Thessalonica, Am-
phipolis, Berea, Philippi, &c. are mentioned in the
New Testament, in which Christianity was founded at
in an early period.

This country was doubtless comprehended under the
term "Chittim," by the prophet Daniel, by which term
he describes Greece in general; and the symbol by
which this nation is designated, that of the "goat
with one horn," (Daniel viii. 5) has been proved,
by reference to medals, coins, and inscriptions of

great antiquity, to have been the ancient symbol proper to Macedonia, as that of Persia was the ram.

No. 1. A representation of an ancient bronze figure of a goat with one horn, which was dug up in Asia Minor. It is supposed to have been affixed to the top of a military standard, in the same manner as the Roman eagle; and it is related in history, that Caranus, the first king of the Macedonians, ordered goats to be carried before the standards of his army.

No. 2. An engraving from a piece of sculpture from a pilaster in the ruins of Persepolis; in which a goat is represented, with a large horn growing out of the middle of his forehead, and a man in a Persian dress is seen by his side, holding the horn with his left hand, by which is signified the subjection of Macedon to Persia, as we have before mentioned in the year 547 before Christ.

No. 3.

No. 3. It has been supposed that the Macedonians derived their origin from Media, and probably thence
brought this symbol of their country, which may once
have been also proper to Media. This plate represents
another sculpture at Persepolis; in which are seen
two single-horned goats, walking together, but each
directed by its proper superintendent; signifying
the two provinces of Upper and Lower Media, subject
to Persia, and under Persian governors.

Other ancient medals represent the head of a ram
joined with the head of a single-horned goat, implying either the united empire of Persia and Media, or
the conquest of Persia by the Macedonians under Alexander.

The fact that both Media and Macedonia were represented by the goat with one horn, explains the reason
of Daniel's perplexity on seeing the vision, as he
could not tell which of the two countries was intended as the conqueror of Persia, until he was informed.

If Persia was represented by a two-horned ram, after
its unification with one-horned Media, then Persia must
have also, originally, been just a one-horned nation;
this deduction would have also given Daniel problems.
And the interpretation confirms the previous one-horned
status of Persia by saying: "The ram which thou sawest
having two horns are the kings of Media and Persia."

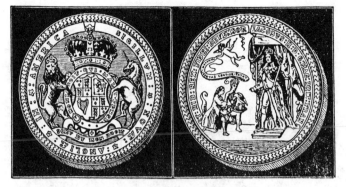

SEAL OF NEW ENGLAND UNDER GOVERNOR ANDROS

The Latin inscriptions read: "Seal of New England in America.
James II by God's grace king of Great Britain, France, and Ireland,
defender of the faith."

Nevertheless, as Persian world power and dominion increased, neither a one-horned wild goat nor a two-horned ram would suffice as an effective royal or stately type of emblem. The national symbol needed to be replaced — with a champion inspiring more respect than a goat. We have a good example of the problem in American history. Though the patriots first served under the noble Unicorn above, they later fought under a hideous coiled serpent when they were in a mean state of rebellion against their British forefathers; but they quickly replaced it with stately stars — which brought the eyes of the people up — as soon as their insurrection had succeeded. A lofty eagle, which, ironically, could easily devour a snake, was shortly emblazoned on the new national seal; and the people then began to feel good about themselves again. The old rebel chiefs in the new regime needed some good old orthodox allegiance in order to control their volatile Puritan confederates. Lawbiding societies usually bear little natural respect for powers symbolized by slippery serpents — let alone rough, hardheaded goats. So our clever Persian predecessors, not altogether unlike our crafty American forefathers, would have had to improve the country's image, considering the exalted status the new state enjoyed then, after so many hard fought military quests — that is, if they wished to rule a very peaceful empire.

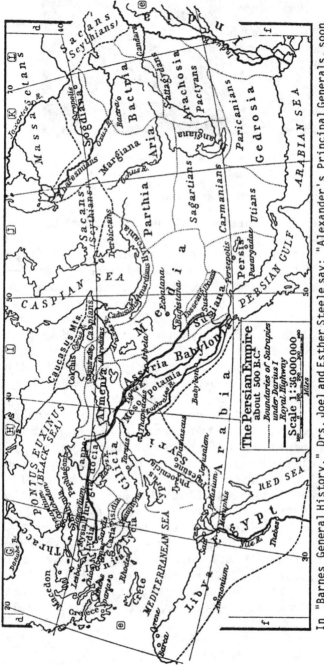

The Persian Empire
about 500 B.C.
.... Boundaries of Satrapies
under Darius I
—— Royal Highway
Scale 1:36000000

In "Barnes General History," Drs. Joel and Esther Steele say: "Alexander's Principal Generals, soon after his death, divided his empire among themselves. . . . and the following distribution of the territory made:—Ptolemy received Egypt, and conquered all of Palestine, Phoenicia, and Cyprus. Lysim'-achus received Thrace and nearly all of Asia Minor. Seleucus received Syria and the East, and he afterward conquered Asia Minor, Lysim'achus being slain. Cassander received Macedon and Greece."

MORE EVIDENCE

For the common soldier, the dirty, unsightly, stubborn ram, or one-horned rough (wild) goat, was an appropriate fighting insignia, but he had served his purpose since Persian victory, power, and dominion over the then known world was already accomplished. Persians were now the world's ruling people, the elite Aryans, and the symbol for the empire demanded universal respect, a peaceful respect, amongst all the conquered nations. Though the Aryan kings — like Cyrus — allowed the defeated races the freedom of worship, it still wasn't enough. Devotion to God was one thing, to Persia, another. There was still a problem: All still revered their old national emblems. The Egyptians and Greeks loved bulls and unicorns; the Macedonians, goats and unicorns; the Assyrians, lions and unicorns; the Babylonians, griffins and unicorns; the Medes, horses and unicorns; and the Persians honored them all — but especially those divine unicorns! The solution was simple: Embrace all their national symbols and inherit all their allegiance. The new Empire Emblems were then proudly proclaimed to the people on the towering monuments and imperial palaces built at Persopolis ("City of the Persians") or Persepolis — as the Greeks liked to call it. But watching over these lower national life-forms, from almost fifty feet above, sat the powerful pride of Persia, the magnificent royal unicorns. "Calmet's Dictionary of the Holy Bible" reports:

> The figure of the unicorn, in various attitudes, is depicted, according to Niebuhr, on almost all the stair-cases found among the ruins of Persepolis. One of these figures is given in vol. ii. plate xxiii. of Niebuhr's Travels; and also in vol. i. p. 594, 595, of the Travels of Sir R. K. Porter. The latter traveller supposes it to be the representation of a bull with a single horn.

The view of the palaces at Persepolis, the platform plan of the royal edifices, and the drawings and measurements of the columns on the next page are provided by Sir Banister Fletcher. In his "History of Architecture on the Comparative Method," he aptly illustrates and describes this imperial home of the unicorns as follows:

The **Palace platform, Persepolis (A, C)** is a remarkable structure, 1,500 ft. by 1,000 ft. in extent and 40 ft. above the plain, partly hewn out of the solid rock and partly built up of large blocks of local stone laid without mortar, but held together by metal clamps. The approach on the northwest was by a magnificent flight of steps, 22 ft. wide, shallow enough for horses to ascend. The **Propylaea (C)** built by Xerxes (BC 485-465) formed a monumental entrance, flanked by man-headed bulls and massive piers glowing in glazed bricks, and through this gateway passed foreign ambassadors, subject princes, and royal retinues to the palaces on the platform. Among these stood out the **"Hall of the Hundred Columns"** built by Darius (B.C. 521-485), which according to Plutarch, was burnt by Alexander the Great. It was probably the audience hall or throne room of the palace and was 225 ft. square, enclosed by brick wall, 11 ft. thick, in which there were some 44 doorways and windows. The walls flanking the entrance portico were enlivened with topical bas-reliefs representing the king with his retinue receiving ambassadors. The flat cedar roof was supported upon 100 columns, 37 ft. high, of which only one remains "in situ," and they recall the hypostyle halls of Egyptian temples, but have a character all their own with moulded bases, fluted shafts, and curious, complex capitals with vertical Ionic-like volutes and twin bulls supporting the roof-beams **(B,D)**. The **Palace of Darius (C)**, the earliest built on the platform, was rectangular in plan with a portico of sixteen columns. The stone lintels and jambs of doors and windows, as well as the bases of the portico columns, still exist, though the rubble walls have crumbled away. The **Palace of Xerxes** (B.C. 485) **(C)**, though it consisted only of a central hall and three columned porticoes, was of great size, with an area of some 24,000 square ft. The Palace was further raised on a podium 10 ft. high, reached by four flights of steps. Columns of porticoes and hall, which originally numbered seventy-two, though only seventeen remain, were 65 ft. high with bell-shaped bases and fluted shafts. Those of the north

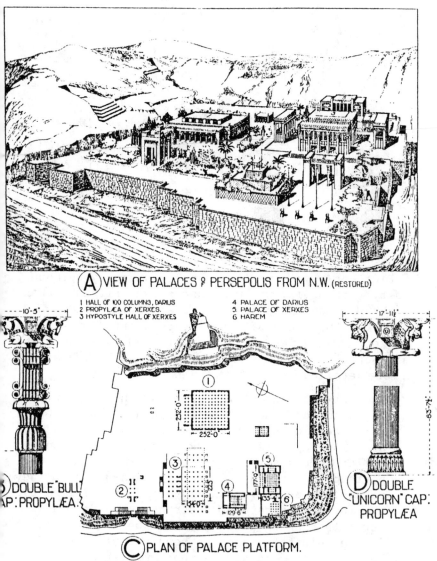

(A) VIEW OF PALACES ♀ PERSEPOLIS FROM N.W. (RESTORED)

1 HALL OF 100 COLUMNS, DARIUS
2 PROPYLÆA OF XERXES.
3 HYPOSTYLE HALL OF XERXES

4 PALACE OF DARIUS
5 PALACE OF XERXES
6 HAREM

(B) DOUBLE "BULL" CAP. PROPYLÆA.

(D) DOUBLE "UNICORN" CAP. PROPYLÆA

(C) PLAN OF PALACE PLATFORM.

portico and great hall had elaborate capitals of Ionic volutes set on end and surmounted by double bulls,
while those of the east and west porticoes consisted
only of double bulls or griffins. Flower gardens,
orange groves, and summer pavilions formed the lux-
urious surroundings of all the palaces of Darius and
Xerxes at Persepolis.

Fig. 56. Details of Persian Architecture.

Fletcher says sometimes the "columns were surmounted by twin bulls, unicorns, horses, or griffins, on the backs of which were placed the cross-beams of the roof."

In his "Outlines of the History of Art," Dr. Wilhelm Lübke, Professor at the Polytechnic Institute and at the Art School in Stuttgart, gives us (in his Fig. 56 above) a more detailed look at them and explains that:

The form of the columns with their high bases (Fig. 56, b and c), the slender, elegantly formed shafts with their deep flutings, point to Ionic-Greek models. The capitals alone show, it seems, a design peculiar to Persia. They are either formed of two foreparts of bulls or unicorns (Fig. 56 a and d), or they consist of an upright and inverted cup (Fig. 56, c), the former decorated with strings of beads, the latter with hanging petals, and the whole crowned with double volutes, placed perpendicularly instead of horizontally — an arrangement which shows a fantastic resemblance to Ionic forms, and thus early foreshadows the elements of a later decorative period. Other forms, again, pointing to Egyptian influences, are to be found in the crowning of the portals (Fig. 56, e), the principal of which exhibits the high Egyptian corona, with three rows of upright leaves covered with a heavy slab.

A ROYAL PERSIAN UNICORN BEING DEVOURED BY A DEVILISH LION — See 1 PETER 5:8. (From Shepard — taken from R. K. Porter's "Travels in Georgia, Persia, etc.")

This theme is repeated on the reliefs of the Processional stairways at Persepolis. Notice the spiraled (whirlwind) horn, and band around the unicorn's neck — See Job.

"PART OF THE ROCK-CUT FACADE OF THE TOMB OF DARIUS"
(From Mrs. Aruthur Bell's "History of Art")

In her "History of Art," Mrs. Bell agrees with Lübke on
the origin of Ionic-Greek columns, and she points out:
"Unicorns are of frequent occurrence in Persian sculptures." They watch over the Persian kings from atop the
columns of their rock tombs and even grace the corners of
the altars above these final resting places. She says:

> The ruins of the immense hexastyle Hall of Xerxes,
> the "Chehil Minar," show that it must have been one of
> the largest buildings in this part of the world. The
> bases of no less than seventy-two columns still re-
> main to mark the enormous size of this grand tem-
> ple, which must have occupied more ground than most
> of the cathedrals of modern times: it was a consid-
> erable height.
> Here also occur the tombs of the Persian monarchs,
> excavated from the rock and adorned with high sculp-
> tured façades also cut from the rock. The "Tomb of
> Darius" at Naksh-i-Rustam is remarkable for having
> on the façade beneath the sarcophagus a representa-
> tion of the Palace of Persepolis as it was in the days
> of the Great King, by means of which the parts missing
> in the ruins can be supplied. In all these façades we
> recognize an imitation of the Persian columns, which

THE ROYAL PERSIAN TOMBS OF NAKSH-I-RUSTAM
(From Dr. James Henry Breasted's "Ancient Times")

are remarkable for the carved bulls' and unicorns' heads which form the capitals, and for the spiral ornament which reappeared at a later date as the characteristic feature of Greek Ionic architecture.

These are the tombs of the Persian kings who ruled after Cyrus, and his son Cambyses. They were excavated in the face of a cliff about six miles from the ruins of Persepolis. In the drawing above, from left to right, are the tombs of Darius II, Antaxerxes I, Darius I (the Great), and Xerxes (at the far end). Besides Cyrus, who is buried elsewhere, and his son Cambyses, whose tomb has never been found, the rest of the Achaemenian line were buried in tombs cut in the cliff behind the palaces of Persepolis. Inside, in niches, are the massive stone coffins in which the kings and their families were buried, but not much else remains. All of these tombs were broken into and robbed long ago.

We can not help but notice the huge crosses enclosing the front of the royal tombs — giving further evidence that the belief in a coming Savior, Jesus, existed long before his arrival — even among the Aryan royalty who avowed to be the very descendants of the gods. Similar rock-cut tombs with crosses are found at Myra in Lycia.

THE ROYAL TOMB OF DARIUS I
(From Fletcher's "History of Architecture")

Below the vigilant unicorns in Bell's partial drawing of the tomb of Darius I (522-486 B.C.), around the doorway in the center of the cross, appear numerous lines of writing. This is the only one of the four tombs with an inscription. It is written in three languages: Persian, Babylonian, and the Sumerian of ancient Susa. According to Reuben Levy, Lecturer in Persian in the University of Cambridge, the first two paragraphs read:

> A great god is Auramazda, who created this earth, who created yonder heaven, who created man, who created welfare for man, who made Darius king, one king of many, one lord of many.
> I am Darius the great king, king of kings, king of the countries possessing all kinds of people, king of this great earth, far and wide, son of Hystaspes, the Achaemenid, a Persian, the son of a Persian, and Aryan, of Aryan descent.

THE UNICORN CANOPY OVER THE PERSIAN THRONE
(At Persepolis — From Rawlinson)

The Aryans of Persia have long lived in the same area, east of Mesopotamia, where the Sumerians, the inventors of the first written language, originally settled many years before. In fact, they even used the old Sumerian (and Elamite) site of Susa (biblical "Shushan") to build the new Persian capital of "Susa" on. And Cyrus, an Aryan Persian — not a Semitic Hebrew — was the Lord Jehovah's "anointed" who believed in the same Creator and God the Father that the Hebrews knew. Cyrus was the great king who freed the Hebrews from Babylonian captivity in the latter part of Daniel's time, to return to Jerusalem to rebuild their temple. It is not unlikely that his royal line descended directly from that puzzling, but highly intelligent, Sumerian race, of which nobody knows the exact origin or destination. But we do know it was not a Semitic race. Most historians and archaeologists now seem to agree on this point. In his "Missing Links Discovered in Assyrian Tablets," E. Raymond Capt, M.A., A.I.A., F.S.A., Scot., verifies the common consensus among the experts. He points out that the Sumerian records reach back to the "remotest times," and that:

Although they appear to be ethnically members of the Great White Race, the Sumerians were not Semitic (an ethnological usage for a branch of the Caucasian or white race) and show no relationship to the Semitic nomads of the Arabian Desert who overran Mesopotamia by the year 3500 B.C. The Sumerians were not descended from the Biblical Adamic branch, starting about 5400 B.C., because evidence (artifacts) of their culture has been found dating many centuries earlier.

MORE EVIDENCE

On the last page is a good close-up of three of the four tombs of Darius and his royal line. The bottom of the crosses are about 30 feet from the ground, and the central ledge at the base of the lateral limbs of each of the crosses support four columns, all crowned with majestic Persian unicorns. At near ground level, between the second and third cross, is a sculpture of a later Persian king, Sapor, of the Sassanian dynasty (A.D. 224-642) who regarded themselves as true heirs of the Achaemenides. In A.D. 260 Sapor succeeded in capturing the Roman Emperor Valerian, who had led an expedition against him in Syria. The relief shows the mounted king receiving the submission of two Romans, the one kneeling is identified as Valerian. On the horse's belly is a Greek and a Pehlevi (middle Persian) royal inscription. The Persian was rendered by Sylvestre de Sacy, a noted French Oriental scholar and Pehlevi translator, as follows:

> The figure of the servant of Ormuzd, of the divine (or god) Ardeshir, king of kings of Iran and An Iran —of the race of the gods, — son of the god Babec, a king.

This is important testimony that, with countless other reports of the fleshy existence of the gods recorded in the Bible and elsewhere, marks the origin of the Aryans. It is their renowned offspring, "the children of light," who still teach the world the ancient Godly precepts, as well as the divine symbolic significance of the Unicorn.

In the fourth edition of his work "Persia, the Land of the Magi," or "The Home of the Wise Men," Samuel Nweeya, M.D., Ph.D., submitted four translations, all done by M. de Sacy, of inscriptions found chiseled in large stone monuments in Persia. We now offer the other three. The first is from Naksh e Rejib, and the last two are from Tauk e Bostam — all harmonize with the testimony above:

> This is the resemblance of the servant of Ormuzd, the divine Shapoor, king of the kings of Iran and An Iran, — of the race of the gods — son of the servant Ormuzd, the divine Artaxares, king of the kings of Iran, — of the race of the gods, — grandson of the divine Babec, the king.

A RELIEF OF CYRUS, THE HEAVENLY SEED OF THE RACE OF GODS
"I am Cyrus, the King, the Achaemenide!"

This is the figure of the adorer of Ormuzd, the excellent Shapoor, king of kings, of Iran and An Iran, — celestial germ of the race of gods, — son of the servant of Ormuzd, the excellent Hoormuz, king of kings, of Iran and An Iran, — celestial germ of the race of the gods, grandson of the excellent Narses, king of kings.

He of whom this is the figure is the adorer of Ormuzd, the excellent Vaharam, king of kings, of Iran and An Iran, — celestial germ of the race of gods, — son of the adorer of Ormuzd, the excellent Sapor, king of kings, of Iran and An Iran, — celestial germ of the race of the gods, — grandson of the excellent Hoormuz, king of kings.

The portrait above shows the Lord's "anointed," Cyrus (Isa. 45:1) — or as the Greeks say: the "Great King." In discussing Cyrus's tomb at Pasargada, and the above,

Lübke says the decoration and "all marks of the burial of Cyrus have disappeared, but his portrait is preserved, singularly enough, upon one of the piers of the palace which lies in ruins, and is thus designated by a contemporaneous cuneiform inscription, 'I am Cyrus, the king, the Achaemenide.'" Note the Trinity symbols — eternal circles or globes, and the spiral, unicorn type of horns on the king's head — and the wings he wears. All these show that Cyrus truly belongs to the race of the gods.

After reading all these royal inscriptions, we cannot doubt that the Aryan kings believed themselves to be the descendants of the gods; and after all, who should know more about these divine matters than the flesh and blood of the gods themselves? We are in no better position today to disregard what our forefathers attested to about the gods than was the honorable Plato (427-347 BC), although he lived thousands of years closer to the facts. Being a Greek, he probably did not receive the record of the gods set down by the Hebrew patriarchs, prophets, priests, and kings — and Christ's testament was not yet available — but he had accepted other ancient testimony that also radiates a sweet aroma of truth; so we happily bow to the temptation to duplicate its savor here:

> To know or tell the origin of the other divinities is beyond us, and we must accept the traditions of the men of old time who affirm themselves to be the offspring of the gods — that is what they say — and they must surely have known their own ancestors. How can we doubt the word of the children of the gods? Although they give no probable or certain proofs, still, as they declare that they are speaking of what took place in their own family, we must conform to custom and believe them. In this manner, then, according to them, the genealogy of these gods is to be received and set forth.
>
> Oceanus and Tethys were the children of Earth and Heaven, and from these sprang Phorcys and Cronos and Rhea, and all that generation; and from Cronos and Rhea sprang Zeus and Herè, and all those who are said to be their brethren, and others who were the children of these.

ZEUS — A GREEK GOD

Now, when all of them, both those who visibly appear in their revolutions as well as those other gods who are of a more retiring nature, had come into being, the creator of the universe addressed them in these words: "Gods, children of gods, who are my works, and of whom I am the artificer and father, my creations are indissoluble, if so I will. All that is bound may be undone, but only an evil being would wish to undo that which is harmonious and happy. Wherefore, since ye are but creatures, ye are not altogether immortal and indissoluble, but ye shall certainly not be dissolved, nor be liable to the fate of death, having in my will a greater and mightier bond than those which ye were bound at the time of your birth. And now listen to my instructions: — Three tribes of mortal beings remain to be created — without them the universe will be incomplete, for it will not contain

every kind of animal which it ought to contain, if
it is to be perfect. On the other hand, if they were
created by me and received life at my hands, they
would be on an equality with the gods. In order then
that they may be mortal, and that this universe may be
truly universal, do ye, according to your natures,
betake yourselves to the formation of animals, imi-
tating the power which was shown by me in creating
you. The part of them worthy of the name immortal,
which is called divine and is the guiding principle
of those who are willing to follow justice and you —
of that divine part I will myself sow the seed, and
having made a beginning, I will hand the work over to
you. And do ye then interweave the mortal with immortal, and make and beget living creatures, and give
them food, and make them to grow, and receive them
again in death."

To close out this chapter and prepare for the next, we
will now quote some of the ancient accounts of unicorns,
which have drifted down to us from the Greek and Roman
writers, and then move on to the Renaissance Period. The
variation in the ancient reports indicates that these
writers were certainly describing different species of
unicorns. "Aristotle knew of only two unicorns," says
Odell Shepard, "but Aelian and Pliny between them muster
seven: the rhinoceros, the Indian ass, the oryx, the
Indian ox, the Indian horse, the bison, and the unicorn
proper and 'par excellence.'" Herodotus, the "Father of
History," (484-425 B.C.), a Persian subject, mentions
"horned asses," from the eastern side of Libya where
the wanderers live, which may be the first reference by
a Greek writer to animals that could have been unicorns.
However, we will begin our chronology of reports with a
more precise and far less speculative quotation from:

CTESIAS (Fifth century B.C.) — A Greek physician to the
Persian court of Artaxerxes and Darius II, who says:

There are in India certain wild asses which are as
large as horses, and larger. Their bodies are white,

their heads dark red, and their eyes dark blue. They have a horn on the forehead which is about a foot and a half in length. The dust filed from this horn is administered in a potion as protection against drugs. The base of this horn, for some two hands'-breath above the brow, is pure white; the upper part is sharp and of a vivid crimson; and the remainder, or middle portion, is black. Those who drink out of these horns, made into drinking vessels, are not subject, they say, to convulsions or to the holy disease. Indeed, they are immune even to poisons if, either before or after swallowing such, they drink wine, water, or anything else from these beakers. Other asses, both the tame and the wild, and in fact all animals with solid hoofs, are without the ankle-bone and have no gall in the liver, but these have both the ankle-bone and the gall. This ankle-bone, the most beautiful I have ever seen, is like that of an ox in general appearance and in size, but it is as heavy as lead and its color is that of cinnabar through and through. The animal is exceedingly swift and powerful, so that no creature, neither the horse nor any other, can overtake it.

There is no other way to capture them in the hunt than this: when they conduct their young to pasture, if they are surrounded by many horsemen, they refuse to flee, thus forsaking their offspring. They fight with thrusts of horn; they kick, bite, and strike with wounding force both horses and hunters; but they perish under the blows of arrows and javelins, for they cannot be taken alive. The flesh of this animal is so bitter that it is not edible; it is hunted for its horn and its ankle-bone.

ARISTOTLE (384-322 B.C.) —— This famous Greek philosopher, who tutored Alexander the Great, says:

There are . . . some animals that have one horn only, for example, the oryx, whose hoof is cloven, the Indian ass, whose hoof is solid. These creatures have their horn in the middle of their head.

EUPHRONIUS'S GREEK ONE-HORNED CATTLE OF GERYON
(From Helen Gardner's "Art Through the Ages")

<u>JULIUS CAESAR</u> (100-44 B.C.) — This great general, orator, statesman, and writer reported the existence of a one-horned animal in the Hercynian forest of Germany:

> There is no man . . . we know who can say that he has reached the edge of that forest, though he may have gone forward a sixty days' journey. . . . It is known that many kinds of wild beasts not seen in other places breed therein, of which the following are those that differ most from the rest of the animal world and appear worthy of record. There is an ox shaped like a stag, from the middle of whose forehead, between the ears, stands forth a single horn, taller and straighter than the horns we know.

<u>PLINY</u>, "the Elder" (23-79 A.D.) — This renowned Roman scholar who wrote many books in the fields of history, rhetoric, science, and military tactics, says:

> The Orsaean Indians hunt an exceedingly wild beast called the monoceros, which has a stag's head, elephant's feet, and a boar's tail, the rest of its body being like that of a horse. It makes a deep lowing noise, and one black horn two cubits long projects from the middle of its forehead. This animal, they say, cannot be taken alive.

<u>AELIAN</u> (c. 170-235 A.D.) — This Roman naturalist says:

> I have found that wild asses as large as horses are to be seen in India. The body of this animal is white,

A 'RHODIAN' VASE WITH ONE-HORNED RAMS
(From "A Handbook of Greek Archaeology")

except on the head, which is red, while the eyes are azure. It has a horn on the brow, about one cubit and half in length, which is white at the base, crimson at the top, and black between. These variegated horns, I learn, are used as drinking-cups by the Indians — although not, to be sure, by all of the people. Only the great men use them, after having them ringed about with hoops of gold exactly as they would put bracelets on some beautiful statue. And it is said that whosovever drinks from this kind of horn is safe from all incurable diseases such as convulsions and the so-called holy disease, and that he cannot be killed by poison.

They say that there are mountains in the interior regions of India which are inaccessible to men and therefore full of wild beasts. Among these is the unicorn, which they call the "cartazon." This animal is as large as a full-grown horse, and it has a mane, tawny hair, feet like those of the elephant, and the tail of a goat. It is exceedingly swift of foot. Between its brows there stands a single black horn, not smooth but with certain natural rings, and tapering to a very sharp point. . . . It is armed besides with an unconquerable horn. . . . No one remembers the capture of a single specimen of mature age.

It is noteworthy to mention here that Aelian spoke of one-horned bulls in Ethiopia; and Pliny spoke of unicorn cattle living in the land of the Moors. And Odell Shepard claims "the mysterious one-horned ox mentioned three times over in the 'Talmud' as Adam's sacrifice to Jehovah may have been the most precious thing that Adam possessed, the leader of his herd of cattle." And he adds later in his work that the sacred writings of Persia affirm that "We worship the Good Mind and the spirits of the Saints and that sacred beast the Unicorn."

"Who is this Unicorn," wrote St. Ambrose, "but the only begotten Son of God." "The unconquerable nature of God is likened to that of a unicorn," wrote Saint Basil. And in his work titled "Tracing Our Ancestors," Frederick Habermann held that the Unicorn is an emblem of the separated kingdom of northern Israel. Yet others maintain that the unicorn stands for the Hebrew people as a whole, "its one horn standing for their single law where-with they are to toss aside all other nations."

During the late Middle Ages, the rapid increase in the printing and reading of the Scriptures, with their clear references to the Unicorn, inspired the medieval lords to often move him off their stationery and tableware onto their crests, shields, and coats of arms that could be flashed in state processions and used to rally soldiers to battle. "The frequent use of the Unicorn would do much to increase the animal's vogue and to make it seem certain, if there had even been any doubt," says Shepard, "that he was as real as any beast of field or forest."

"The UNICORN," declares E. Raymond Capt, "holds a very important place in the heraldry of the Celto-Saxon peoples. It is one of the two supporters in the heraldry of the Royal Arms of Britain. In the Arms of Scotland, both supporters are UNICORNS. The UNICORN also appears in the Arms of Preton of Craigmiller; on the Crests of Ramsay, Earl of Dalhousis; Cunningham, Earl of Glencarirn; Lord

THE ROYAL STEWARD ARMS OF SCOTLAND
"My horn shalt thou exalt like the horn of an unicorn"

Oliphant, and as supporters in the Arms of the Chief of Clan Steward" —— whence arose the Royal Arms of Charles James Steward, the Scottish King, who gave the world's English speaking peoples "THE HOLY BIBLE, Containing the Old Testament and the New: Newly Translated out of the Original tongues: and with the former Translations diligently compared and revised: by his Majesty's Special Commandment. Appointed to be read in Churches."

At the end of his Assyrian work, E. Raymond Capt says: "King James VI of Scotland (King James I of England) claimed that the Lord had made him 'King over Israel' and upon the gold coin of his day, (the Jacobus) he had inscribed in Latin the prophecy of Ezekiel 37:22 'I will make of them one nation.'" And just before he had stepped up to the English throne, to become the first King of Great Britian, Queen Elizabeth's godson Lord Harington wrote: "God for His house a Steward hath provided."

I V

CHAPTER FOUR

R E C E N T   E V I D E N C E

In an illustrated study printed in Germany in 1486, Bernhard von Breydenbach, a deacon in Mainz Cathedral, verbally and graphically detailed, with the help of the Dutch artist Erhard Reuwich, the sights and inhabitants encountered by a congregation of pilgrims on a trip to the Middle East. Breydenbach faithfully compiled his 148 page exposition entitled "Peregrinatio in Terram Sanctam," better rendered: "Travel to the Holy Land," after he had led his flock in 1483 on a lengthy excursion from Venice to Jaffa, on to Ramla by caravan, and finally into Jerusalem for an extended visit to all the holy sites. They also ventured west into the forbidding Sinai Desert to the Monastery of Santa Catharina, and a member of that pilgrimage, Felix Fabri, "saw, on September 20, 1483, with his own eyes — as did all the members of his company — a unicorn standing on a hill near Mt. Sinai, and he observed it carefully for a long time." Breydenbach then continued onward to the Red Sea, into Cairo, and back to Europe. His popular travel documentary was translated from Latin into many languages, and its numerous editions were eagerly sought after by people of many nations for hundreds of years thereafter. "This is the earliest illustrated book of travel," says Odell Shepard. "The drawings for the woodcuts, which are numerous and excellent, were made from nature by Erhard Reuwich of Utrecht, who was one of the 150 members of the pilgrimage. This artist must have been one of the company who saw the unicorn described by Felix Fabri in

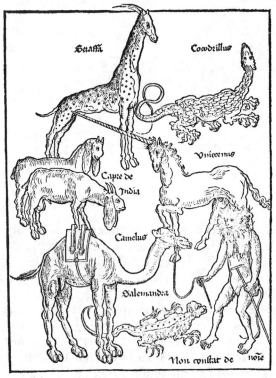

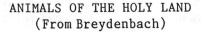

ANIMALS OF THE HOLY LAND
(From Breydenbach)

the book he wrote about the same expedition, and it was probably on the strength of that observation that he included the unicorn among the beasts 'truthfully depicted as we saw them in the Holy Land.'"

The above is a reduced facsimile of one of Reuwich's woodcuts, which covered a whole page in Breydenbach's book, published in 1486 — of which Erhard "carried out the printing in his own house." It portrays the spiral-horned unicorn among other creatures from the Holy Land. Included are the crocodile, giraffe, and camel. The bizarre images of these strange beasts probably shocked European readers much more than the already familiar unicorn — which looked much like a common horse anyway.

They were scarcely known in Europe at the time the book was published. The animal holding the rope is similar to the one Layard thought might be the Wanderoo or Maned Ape — portrayed along with a bull, a unicorn, an antelope, an elephant, camels, and some monkeys on the obelisk discovered among the ancient ruins of Nimrûd. The Latin at the foot of the page translates: "These animals are truthfully depicted as we saw them in the Holy Land."

"The most important of all descriptions of the unicorn given by the few who claim to have seen the animal is that of Lewis Vartoman (Ludovico Barthema), of Bologna, who travelled in 1503 through the countries of the Near East," says Odell Shepard. "At the city of Zeila in Ethiopia he saw certain cattle with single horns about a palm and a half in length rising from their brows and bending backward, but much more important than these were the unicorns in a park adjoining the temple at Mecca. There were two of these animals,"

showed to the people for a miracle, and not without reason for the seldomness and strange nature. The one of them, which is much higher than the other, yet not much unlike to a colt of thirty months of age, in the forehead groweth only one horn, in a manner right forth, of the length of three cubits. The other is much younger, of the age of one year, and like a young colt: the horn of this is of the length of four handfuls. This beast is of the colour of a horse of weasel colour, and hath the head like an hart, but no long neck, a thin mane hanging only on the one side. Their legs are thin and slender, like a fawn or hind. The hoofs of the forefeet are divided in two, much like the feet of a Goat. The outward part of the hinder feet is very full of hair. This beast doubtless seemeth wild and fierce, yet tempereth that fierceness with a certain comeliness. These Unicorns one gave to the Sultan of Mecca as a most precious and rare gift. They were sent him out of Ethiopia by a king of that Country, who desired by that present to gratify the Sultan of Mecca.

"I have seen," says oriental traveler Vincent Le Blanc in 1567, "a unicorn in the seraglio of the Sultan, others in India, and still others at the Escurial. That there are some persons who doubt whether this animal is to be found anywhere in the world I am well aware, but in addition to my own observation there are several serious writers who bear witness to its existence — Vartoman among others, who says that he saw some at the same place."

Mr. Odell Shepard, the twentieth-century authority on unicorns, says Vincent Le Blanc "saw only one unicorn at Mecca, the other one mentioned by Vartoman having died, but by way of atonement he saw two at the Court of Pegu." This means the surviving unicorn at Mecca had to be, at least, in his sixties by the time Vincent saw him; so we now know the normal longevity of a healthy unicorn could be great.

"I have seen," wrote the Elizabethan traveler Edward Webbe in 1590, "in a place like a Park adjoining unto Prester John's Court, three score and seventeen unicorns and elephants all alive at one time, and they were so tame that I have played with them as one would play with young lambs."

These relatively recent eyewitness reports are not the only particulars confirming the reality of unicorns. Trustworthy descriptions of the famous unicorn horns preserved in some of the great European cathedrals and royal treasure-houses of the seventeenth century, given by religious men with a good reputation, also bear witness. One of the horns belonged to the British Solomon, King James I, who ordained the great 1611 Authorized Translation of the Bible. He stepped up to the British throne in 1603, and four years later Edward Topsell published his celebrated natural "Historie of Foure-footed Beastes" — the very catalyst that popularized modern-day zoology. Its 816 pages are beautifully illuminated with ornamental pieces, many illustrations throughout the text, and a table of names of all the beasts "in divers languages" at the end. Eleven pages are devoted to the Unicorn, and another three to the one-horned oryx. This renowned reference was used by Shakespeare, and it was a delight to Christians, who drew so many moral lessons from its descriptions. Under the large heading "Of the Vnicorne," with a picture of the creature beneath (reproduced here on the following page), Reverend Topsell, Chaplain in the Church of St. Botolph, Aldersgate, gives us his detailed description of the famous unicorn horn kept with the Crown Jewels and King James's other royal regalia at the old Tower of London:

> I do also know, that which the King of England possesseth to be wreathed in spires, even as that is accounted in the Church of S. Dennis, then which they suppose to be none greater in the world, and I never saw any thing in any creatures more worthy of praise than this horn. . . . It is of so great a length, that the tallest man can scarcely touch the top thereof, for it doth fully equal seven great feet. It weigheth thirteen pounds with their assize, being only weighed by the guess of the hand, it seemeth much heavier. The figure doth plainly signify a wax candle, (being folded and wreathed within itself) being far more thicker from one part, and making itself by little and little less towards the point, the thickest part thereof cannot be shut within one's hand, it is the compass of five fingers, by the circumference, if it be measured with a thread, it is three fingers and a span.
>
> That part, which is next unto the head hath no sharpness, the other are of a polished smoothness. The splints of the spire are smooth and not deep, being for the most part like unto the wreathing turnings of Snails, or the revolutions or windings of Wood-bine about any wood. But they proceed from the right hand toward the left, from the beginning of the horn, even unto the very end. The colour is not altogether white, being a long time somewhat obscured. But by the weight it is an easy thing to conjecture, that this beast which can bear so great a burden in his head, in the quantity of his body can be little less than a great Ox.

OF THE VNICORNE.

THE UNICORN OR "GREAT OX"
(From Topsell's History of Four-Footed Beasts)

The unicorn horn at the Tower that Topsell had seen had mysteriously disappeared by 1662. Nobody knows exactly what happened to it, but Dr. Thomas Fuller gives us a dark clue under the heading "The Unicorn Horn" in his famed "Worthies of England." "Amongst the many precious rarities in the Tower," he wrote at the beginning of his piece, "this (as another in Windsor castle) was, in my memory, shewn to people. It belongs not to me to inquire what is become of them." Yet, at the end of his article he tells us that Dr. Hamey took another that looked like a taper of wreathed wax "to the college of physicians; and they have solemnly presented this unicorn's horn to His Majesty, to supply the place of that in the Tower, which our civil wars have embezzled."

RECENT EVIDENCE

The other horn just mentioned by Fuller, in Windsor castle, was the great "Horn of Windsor," says Shepard:

> which the German traveller Hentzner saw in 1598 and valued, if his Latin text is to be trusted, at one hundred thousand pounds. We know exactly when and where this horn was discovered; it was picked up on the twenty-second of July, 1577, on an island in Frobisher's Strait, and we are told that when it reached England it was "reserved as a jewell by the Queen's Majesty's commandment, in her wardrobe of robes."

Thomas Fuller's "History of the Worthies of England" was first published back in 1662, and it is still being reprinted over 300 years later. One of the reasons this work has enjoyed such immense popularity is because of the quaint little descriptions he gives of such things as unicorn horns, in his quite charming, but slightly pedantic, seventeenth-century style:

> Come we now to the fashion and colour of the horn, conceiving it no considerable controversy concerning the length and bigness thereof, quantity not varying the kind in such cases. Some are plain, as that in St. Mark's in Venice; others wreathed about, as that at St. Dyonis near Paris, with anfractuous spires, and cocleary turnings about it, which probably is the effect of age, those wreaths being but the wrinkles of most vivacious unicorns. The same may be said of the colour; white, when newly taken from his head; yellow, like that lately in the Tower, of some hundred years seniority; but whether or no it will ever turn black, as that of Aelian's and Pliny's description, let others decide.

A careful researcher has noted some curious details about the turnings or whirls of alicorns (unicorn horns) depicted so often in medieval pictures. It is noteworthy to point out that some of these works were created almost three centuries before anyone ever saw Erhard Reuwich's woodcut of the spiral-horned unicorn of the Holy Land, portrayed in Breydenbach's book. Shepard says:

> By far the strangest thing in the history of opinion about the alicorn's appearance is the age and persistence of the belief in the natural spiral twistings or striae. These are clearly delineated in every picture of the unicorn that I have seen in mediaeval manuscripts, some of which were drawn in the twelfth century. It is possible that Aelian meant to describe them in his phrase. . . . Even the horns of the unicorned animals shown in bas-relief on the walls of Persepolis seem to show these twistings. There is nothing said about them, however, in Ctesias, Pliny, Solinus, Isidore, or "Physiologus"; aside from the mysterious passage in Aelian, there seems to be no ancient authority for them whatever, and learned writers do not mention them until after the close of the Middle Ages.

We have not bothered the reader with Aelian's Greek phrase, but replaced it in the quote with ellipses instead. However, Shepard says the Greek could refer to either "rings," or "spirals." This naturally leaves the question in mind: How could the mediaeval artists have been so persistent in drawing the unicorn's horn with "natural spiral twistings," unless they or their acquaintances had actually seen the horn themselves?

Nevertheless, the horn is not the only item attesting to the existence of unicorns. Bones provide even more proof. And once again, Shepard gives us the details:

> In the year 1663 there was discovered in a limestone quarry near Quedlinberg in Germany the "skeleton of a unicorn." We are told that it was crouched upon its hind-quarters with its head thrown back, and that it had on its brow a horn as thick as a human shinbone and seven and a half feet in length. The workmen broke it up and extracted it piece-meal, but the head and horn together with some of the ribs and the spine were handed over to a responsible person and were accurately described.

RECENT EVIDENCE

Perhaps Anne Clark, in her book "Beasts and Bawdy," was reporting on the same discovery when she wrote:

> At Swedenburg in Germany during the year 1663 a heap of bones together with a large horn believed to belong to a unicorn was unearthed. Among those present when the horn was dug up was the mayor of the nearby town of Magdeburg, and his imagination was so captured by the discovery that he tried to reconstruct the skeleton. Partly because it was put together on the assumption that it must resemble known descriptions of the unicorn, the result was extraordinary, but as far as we know this was the oldest recorded attempt at a palaeontological reconstruction.

We will now vary slightly from the order of our chronology, but will still stay on the subject. In his well documented work on unicorns, Mr. Shepard added another interesting report on the discovery, at a later date, of still more unicorn bones in Germany. It reads:

> Somewhat before the middle of the eighteenth century a similar skeleton was found in the so-called Einhornloch at Scharzfeld in the Harz Mountains, and this one was seen and described by no less a person than the philosopher Leibniz. Admitting that recent treatises and discoveries have caused him some doubts in the past concerning the real existence of the unicorn, Leibniz says that the Quedlinberg skeleton and this of Scharzfeld have converted him entirely. He publishes a drawing, intended to represent the reconstruction of the animal, which does not "carry conviction." It is interesting enough, however, to find one of the most brilliant minds of the eighteenth century convinced of the unicorn's existence.

In the 1832 revised edition of "Calmet's Dictionary of the Holy Bible," its editor, Edward Robinson, Professor Extraordinary of Sacred Literature in the Theological Seminary, Andover, reported that

HISTORICAL EVIDENCE FOR UNICORNS

Don Juan Gabriel, a Portuguese colonel, who lived several years in Abyssinia, assures us, that in the region of Agamos in the Abyssinian province of Damota, he had seen an animal of the form and size of a middle-sized horse, of a dark chestnut-brown color, and with a whitish horn about five spans long upon the forehead; the mane and tail were black, and the legs short and slender. Several other Portuguese, who were placed in confinement upon a high mountain in the district Namna, by the Abyssinian king Adamas Saghedo, related that they had seen, at the foot of the mountain, several unicorns feeding. (Ludolf's Hist. Aethiop. lib. i. c. 10. n. 80, seq.) These accounts are confirmed by father Lobo, who lived for a long time as a missionary in Abyssinia. He adds, that the unicorn is extremely shy, and escapes from closer observation by a speedy flight into the forests; for which reason there is no exact description of him. (Voyage histor. d'Abyssinie, Amst. 1728, vol. i. p. 83,291.)

"Lobo left two accounts of Abyssinia," says Shepard, "one of which was translated into French from the unpublished manuscript and out of the French into English by Samuel Johnson in his Grub Street years. This familiar book contains the following passage:"

In the Province of Agaus has been seen the Unicorn, the Beast so much talk'd of and so little known; the prodigious Swiftness with which this Creature runs from one Wood into another has given me no Opportunity of examining it particularly, yet I have had so near sight of it as to be able to give some Description of it. The Shape is the same as that of a beautiful Horse, exact and nicely proportion'd, of a Bay Colour, with a black Tail, which in some Provinces is long, in others very short; some have long Manes hanging to the Ground. They are so Timorous that they never Feed but surrounded with other Beasts that defend them.

"It is pleasant to have this passage in Johnson's phraseology, and one would like to know what the man who kept an open mind about the Cock Lane Ghost thought concerning the unicorn. His 'Dictionary,' I think, forbids us to include him among the believers, but in his Preface to the Lobo translation he says that whatever the Jesuit relates,"

whether true or not, is at least probable; and he who tells nothing exceeding the bounds of probability has a right to demand that they should believe him who cannot contradict him. He appears to have described things as he saw them, to have copied Nature from the Life, and to have consulted his Senses, not his Imagination.

"One is glad to recall Johnson's measured assertion while considering Father Lobo's second passage on this topic, which appears in 'A Short Relation of the River Nile,' edited, or perhaps one may say written, in 1669 by Sir Peter Wyche. The contents of this book are: 'A Short Relation of the River Nile; The True Cause of the River Nile Overflowing; Of the Famous Unicorn: — where He is Bred and how Shaped; The Reason why the Abyssine Emperor is Called Prester John of the Indies; A Short Tract of the Red Sea; A Discourse of Palm-Trees.' All of this is obviously delectable matter, but the best chapter is that concerning 'The Unicorn, the most celebrated among Beasts, as among Birds are the Phoenix, the Pelican, and the Bird of Paradise.' This animal is"

of the more credit because mentioned in the holy Scriptures, compared to many things, even to God made man. None of the Authors who speak of the Unicorn discourse of his birth or Country, satisfied with the deserved eulogiums by which he is celebrated. That secret was reserved for those who travelled and surveyed many countries. . . . The country of the Unicorn (an African creature, only known there) is the Province of Agaos in the kingdom of Damotes; that it may

wander into places more remote is not improbable.
. . . A Father, my companion, who spent some time in
this province, upon notice that this so famous animal
was there, used all diligence to procure one. The
natives brought him a very young colt, so tender as in
a few days it died. A Portuguese Captain, a person
of years and credit, told me that returning once from
the army with twenty other Portuguese soldiers in
company they one morning rested in a little valley
encompassed with thick woods, designing to breakfast
while their horses grazed on the good grass. Scarce
were they sat down when from the thickest part of the
wood lightly sprang a perfect horse of the same colour, hair, and shape before described. His career
was so brisk and wanton that he took no notice of
those new inmates till engaged among them; then, as
frightened at what he had seen, suddenly started back
again, yet left the spectators sufficient time to
see and observe at their pleasure. The particular
survey of these parts seized them with delight and
admiration. One of his singularities was a beautiful
strait horn on his forehead. He appeared to run about
with his eyes full of fear. Our horses seemed to allow
him for one of the same brood, curvetted and made
towards him. The soldiers, observing him in less
than musket shot, not able to shoot, their muskets
being unfixt, endeavoured to encompass him, out of an
assurance that that was the famous unicorn; but he
prevented them, for, perceiving them, with the same
violent career he recovered the wood, leaving the
Portuguese satisfied in the truth of such an animal.
My knowledge of this captain makes the truth with me
undoubted. In another place of the same province (the
most remote, craggy, and mountainous part, called
Manina) the same beast hath been often seen grazing
amongst others of different kinds. . . . To this place
of banishment a tyrannical Emperor named Adamas Se-
gued sent without any cause divers Portuguese, who
from the top of these mountains saw the unicornes
grazing in the plains below, the distance not greater
than allowed them so distinct an observation as they

knew him, like a beautiful Gennet, with a fair horn in his forehead.

The reports of unicorn sightings over the past few centuries are convincing, and Odell Shepard has provided us with a good sample of them — in his heavily researched work titled "The Lore of the Unicorn." However, for the sake of variety, and for further confirmation of what Shepard likewise reports, we will now turn to Professor Robinson for the wrap up of this chapter. He says:

In more recent times we find further traces of the animal in question in Southern Africa. Dr. Sparrmann, the Swedish naturalist, who visited the cape of Good Hope and the adjacent regions in the years 1772-1776, gives, in his travels, the following account: Jacob Kock, an observing peasant on Hippopotamus river, who had travelled over the greater part of Southern Africa, found on the face of a perpendicular rock a drawing made by the Hottentots, representing a quadruped with one horn. The Hottentots told him, that the animal there represented was very like the horse on which he rode, but had a straight horn upon the forehead. They added, that these one-horned animals were rare, that they ran with great rapidity, and were also very fierce. They also described the manner of hunting them. "It is not probable," Dr. Sparrmann remarks, "that the savages wholly invented this story, and that too so very circumstantially: still less can we suppose, that they should have received and retained, merely from history or tradition, the remembrance of such an animal. These regions are very seldom visited; and the creature might, therefore, long remain unknown. That an animal so rare should not be better known to the modern world, proves nothing against its existence. The greater part of Africa is still among the 'terrae incognitae.' Even the 'giraffe' has been again discovered only within comparatively a few years. So also the 'gnu,' which, till recently, was held to be a fable of the ancients."

A somewhat more definite account of a similar animal is contained in the Transactions of the Zealand Academy of Sciences at Flushing. (Pt. xv. Middelb. 1792. Praef. p. lvi.) The account was transmitted to the society in 1791, from the cape of Good Hope, by Mr. Henry Cloete. It states that a bastard Hottentot, Gerrit Slinger by name, related that while engaged several years before with a party, in pursuit of the savage Bushmen, they had got sight of nine strange animals, which they followed on horseback, and shot one of them. This animal resembled a horse, and was of a light-gray color, with white stripes under the lower jaw. It had a single horn, directly in front, as long as one's arm, and at the base about as thick. Towards the middle the horn was somewhat flattened, but had a sharp point; it was not attached to the bone of the forehead, but fixed only in the skin. The head was like that of the horse, and the size also about the same. The hoofs were round, like those of a horse, but divided below, like those of oxen. This remarkable animal was shot between the so-called Table mountain and Hippopotamus river, about sixteen days' journey on horseback from Cambedo, which would be about a month's journey in ox-wagons from Capetown. Mr. Cloete mentions, that several different natives and Hottentots testify to the existence of a similar animal with one horn, of which they profess to have seen drawings by hundreds, made by the Bushmen on rocks and stones. He supposes that it would not be difficult to obtain one of these animals, if desired. His letter is dated at the Cape, April 8, 1791. (See thus far Rosenmüller's Altes u. neues Morgenland, ii. p. 269, seq. Leipz. 1818.)

Such appear to have been the latest accounts of the animal in question, when it was again suddenly brought into notice as existing in the elevated regions of central India. The Quarterly Review for Oct. 1820, (vol. xxiv. p. 120.) in a notice of Frazer's tour through the Himlaya mountains, goes on to remark as follows: "We have no doubt that a little time will bring to light many objects of natural history pe-

culiar to the elevated regions of central Asia, and
hitherto unknown in the animal, vegetable and miner-
al kingdoms, particularly in the two former. This
is an opinion which we have long entertained; but
we are led to the expression of it on the present
occasion, by having been favored with the perusal of
a most interesting communication from major Latter,
commanding in the rajah of Sikkim's territories, in
the hilly country east of Nepaul, addressed to the
adjutant-general Nicol, and transmitted by him to
the marquis of Hastings. This important paper explicitly states that the unicorn, so long considered
as a fabulous animal, actually exists at this moment
in the interior of Thibet, where it is well known to
the inhabitants. 'This' — we copy from the major's
letter — 'is a very curious fact, and it may be nec-
essary to mention how the circumstance became known
to me. In a Thibetian manuscript, containing the
names of different animals, which I procured the
other day from the hills, the 'unicorn' is classed
under the head of those whose hoofs are divided: it
is called the one-horned 'tso'po: Upon inquiring
what kind of animal it was, to our astonishment, the
person who brought the manuscript described exactly
the unicorn of the ancients; saying, that it was a
native of the interior of Thibet, about the size of
a 'tattoo,' (a horse from twelve to thirteen hands
high,) fierce and extremely wild; seldom, if ever,
caught alive, but frequently shot; and that the flesh
was used for food.' — 'The person,' major Latter
adds, 'who gave me this information, has repeatedly
seen these animals, and eaten the flesh of them. They
go together in herds, like our wild buffaloes, and
are very frequently to be met with on the borders
of the great desert, about a month's journey from
Lassa, in that part of the country inhabited by the
wandering Tartars.'

"The communication is accompanied by a drawing made
by the messenger from recollection. It bears some
resemblance to a horse, but has cloven hoofs, a long
curved horn growing out of the forehead, and a boar-

shaped tail, like that of the 'fera monoceros' described by Pliny. From its herding together, as the
unicorn of the Scriptures is said to do, as well as
from the rest of the description, it is evident that
it cannot be the rhinoceros, which is a solitary
animal; besides major Latter states that, in the
Thibetian manuscript, the rhinoceros is described
under the name of 'servo,' and classed with the elephant; 'neither,' says he, 'is it the wild horse,
(well known in Thibet,) for that has also a different name, and is classed in the manuscript with the
animals which have the hoofs undivided.' — 'I have
written,' he subjoins, 'to the Sachia Lama, request-
ing him to procure me a perfect skin of the animal,
with the head, horn and hoofs; but it will be a long
time before I can get it down, for they are not to be
met with nearer than a month's journey from Lassa.'"

As a sequel to this account, we find the following paragraph in the Calcutta Government Gazette,
August, 1821: "Major Latter has obtained the horn
of a young unicorn from the Sachia Lama, which is
now before us. It is twenty inches in length; at the
root it is four inches and a half in circumference,
and tapers to a point; it is black, rather flat at
the sides, and has fifteen rings, but they are only
prominent on one side; it is nearly straight. Major
Latter expects to obtain the head of the animal, with
the hoofs and the skin, very shortly, which will af-
ford positive proof of the form and character of the
'tso'po,' or Thibet unicorn."

"Such are the latest accounts which have reached us
of this animal," added Robinson. "Their credibility
cannot well be contested, and the coincidence of the
description with that of Pliny is so striking." This
learned professor leaves us with little doubt that the
unicorn, as late as the early nineteenth century, did,
in fact, exist. His final words on the subject are:
"The unicorn, at all events, is and was an animal of
exceeding rarity."

CHAPTER FIVE

CURRENT EVIDENCE

In his discourse on unicorns, Edward Topsell readily acknowledged the fact there was a great variety of one-horned creatures in the world — besides his "Vnicorne," shown in our last chapter. He discussed them in detail, and did not hesitate to quote the writers who had seen or heard of them. But, because of the nobleness and virtue ascribed to the unicorn's horn by the ancient writers, Church fathers, and Holy Scriptures, Topsell concluded that there could be just one true (biblical) unicorn.

Edward lived in an age of religious conscientiousness. British Christians daily read their Bible, one of the few books in English that was widely available to all. The Bible said there were unicorns and the Bible spoke the truth! The Bible meant just what it said, nothing more and nothing less! At that time most Christians actually believed the Bible. It was taken seriously. Many even died for it. The Bible spoke the words of God! And the Bible showed the horn was special and sacred — "my horn shalt thou exalt like the horn of an unicorn."

So with the information offered by the Bible, together with trustworthy descriptions from other sources, and his own firsthand knowledge of its horn, he reconstructed the image of "the true Unicorn," which looks similar to the one emblazoned on the British National Arms.

All the others had to be evil imitations. The ancient unicorns of the Near East had not yet been dug up, nor had the cuneiform writing on the monuments been deciphered; so that was not considered. And as a devout Christian, he couldn't allow his pen to ignore these deceptions. Truth demands action. The Devil was blinding the eyes of many of God's people. They were denying a true wonder of God, and falsely delivering their allegiance to other kinds of unicorns, which featured far inferior types of horns.

KING JAMES I'S ROYAL ARMS OF GREAT BRITAIN——1603-1625
——"Evil to him who thinks evil" & "God and my right"——
(From John Guillim's "Display of Heraldry"——1611)

So, with a straightforwardness, not very characteristic of many modern-day clergymen, he didn't hesitate to vigorously condemn those wayward souls. After courteously describing some one-horned animals observed by the ancients, with no mention of any redeeming qualities in their horns, he went on in his discourse (below) to describe some others; but at the end, he let his Christian spirit prevail, and he issued a stern reprimand:

We should as easily believe that there was a Unicorn in the world, as we do believe there is an Elephant, although not bred in Europe. To begin therefore with this discourse, by the Unicorn we do understand a peculiar beast, which hath naturally but one horn, and that a very rich one that groweth out of the middle of the forehead, for we have showed in other parts of the history that there are divers beasts that have but one horn, and namely some Oxen in India have but one horn, and some have three, and whole hooves. Likewise, the Bulls of Aonia are said to have whole hooves and one horn growing out of their foreheads. . . . It is said that Pericles had a ram with one horn . . . Aelianus writeth that there be Birds in Ethiopia having one horn on their foreheads, and therefore are called "Unicornus": and Albertus saith there is a fish called "Monoceros," and it hath also one horn.

Now our discourse of the Unicorn is of none of these beasts, for there is not any virtue attributed to their horns, and therefore the vulgar sort of infidel people which scarcely believe any herb but such as they see in their own Gardens, or any beast but such as is in their own flocks, or any knowledge but such as is bred in their own brains, or any birds which are not hatched in their own Nests, have never made question of these, but of the true Unicorn, whereof there were more proofs in the world, because of the nobleness of his horn, they have ever been in doubt: by which distraction, it appeareth to me that there is some secret enemy in the inward degenerate nature of man, which continually blindeth the eyes of God his people, from beholding and believing the greatness of God his works.

A FOUR-HORNED SHEEP
(From "Wonders of Animal Life")

In Topsell's discourse the ancient writers vouched for some pretty amazing beasts of long ago, but a comparison of the fabulous specimens still alive today makes their testimony very convincing. The photograph above shows a four-horned sheep. This type of sheep was still common in the Hebrides and Iceland in the beginning of this century. Encyclopedia Britannica says that "there is another four-horned breed, distinguished by its black (in place of brown) horns, whose home is probably S. Africa." In India, another animal species is equally represented by the chousingha or four-horned antelope (Tetraceros quadricornis); so Topsell's three-horned oxen, also of India, are easily overshadowed by the extra horn borne by some of today's variety of beasts.

A MODERN UNICORN SHEEP
(From "Wonders of Animal Life")

The photograph of the odd animal above gives even more creditability to the strange beasts cited in Topsell's discourse. He inhabits the rugged highland country of Tibet or Nepal. Only the ram has the horn. It looks like two horns becoming one, or one becoming two, depending on whether we think in terms of a glass being half full or half empty. But he isn't the only anomaly found in those high mountains. Britannica says the Unicorn-antelope ("Budorcas") is an Indo-Malayan form that reaches up into Tibet. That respected authority also mentions the Rhinoceros Bird ("Buceros"), a feathered unicorn found living in nearby India, which "has a crooked horn in the forehead." Pericles's hoary one-horned ram hardly seems strange if we consider these modern species of unicorns.

CURRENT EVIDENCE

It is not hard to believe Aelian's account of the one-horned birds of Ethiopia if we accept the reality of the fabulous flying unicorn shown in the photograph on the opposite page. This bizarre specimen, officially designated the "unicorn bird" or "horned screamer," haunts the jungles of Guiana and the Amazon valley. This bird, which grows to the size of a turkey, is properly classified a unicorn because of the long horny protrusion extending from its crown. It is called a screamer because of the loud and violent noise it makes. It likes to flock together with its friends in the quiet South American lagoons, and when the feathered congregations resolve to scream all together in chorus, the neighborhood is apt to become intolerable. Unfortunately for Topsell, these rowdy birds introduced themselves to the Western world over forty years after he published his work; so they won't be found on his list of unicorns.

But these birds are not the only type of unicorns still found living in the world today, and Albertus was not really wrong when he reported that there is a fish called "Monoceros" which has one horn. Although the whale is now classed as a mammal, it still swims like a fish; and the "Encyclopedia of Sciences" says the swimming unicorn, portrayed on the following page, "is also called 'sea unicorn,' 'unicorn whale,' or 'unicorn fish.'" And "Amies' Universal Encyclopedia" gives us a brief but interesting description of this animal (known also as the narwal, narwhal, and narwhale) that it defines as:

> The "Monodon monoceros," an extraordinary marine animal, which belongs to the "Delphinidae," but differs from the other "Cetacea" in being armed with a formidable horn, projecting directly forward from the upper jaw, in a straight line with the body. This horn is from 6 to 10 feet long, spirally striated throughout its whole length, and tapering to a point; it is harder and whiter than ivory. The N. is from 20 to 30 feet in length from the mouth to the tail, and chiefly inhabits the Arctic seas. It is one of the most peaceable inhabitants of the ocean, feeding, it is said, on the smaller kinds of flatfish.

HISTORICAL EVIDENCE FOR UNICORNS

It is also said that this extraordinary marine animal has one more particular quality, which Amies' Encyclopedia failed to mention. It was confirmed in the latter part of the sixteenth century, as a by-product of Martin Frobisher's voyage to discover a north-west passage. During this voyage his men inadvertently discovered, according to Master Dionise Settle:

> A dead fish floating, which had in his nose a horn straight and torquet, of length two yards lacking two inches, being broken in the top, where we might perceive it hollow — into the which our sailors putting spiders, they presently died. I saw not the trial thereof, but it was reported to me of a truth, by the virtue whereof we suppose it to be the sea-unicorne.

The spider-test confirmed that the horn was a product that was "good against poison." Along with the land-unicorn, the ground up horn of the sea unicorn was then becoming a popular neutralizing agent for poisons, but the genuine antidote was rare and expensive because the market was becoming very lucrative. Royalty had always nurtured the fear of being poisoned, and Mary Queen of Scots, a martyr for the Catholic Church, was no exception. Long before her tragic end, while she was lingering in one of Queen Elizabeth's prisons, the fear manifested itself in a letter she wrote to the Archbishop of Glasgow in May of 1574. Her postscript embraced the following plea:

> I beg you to send me some genuine "terra sigillata," if it is to be had for money, if not, ask M. the Cardinal, my uncle, for some; or, if he has none, rather than have recourse to the Queen, my mother-in-law, or to the King, a bit of fine unicorn's horn, as I am in great want of it.

Her son James VI saw an even greater virtue in the unicorn than this antidote. After he ascended to the English throne to unite Scotland and England in the person of James I, the first king of Great Britain promptly

THE SEA UNICORN
(From "The Living Animals of the World")

dismissed the hideous dragon Elizabeth had on the Royal
Arms, and replaced it with a majestic unicorn instead.
The Unicorn still stands — a symbol of Great Britain.

AN ENORMOUS UNICORN
(From "The Living Animals of the World")

A much less majestic unicorn is the Indian Rhinoceros. After the elephant, he is the largest land mammal of the East. Though he appears to be smiling, he is probably not happy at all. The stub between his eyes tells the story. When successfully held in captivity, and they rarely are, this high-spirited type of unicorn apparently becomes very frustrated, and rubs his face against any hard surface that he can use. Then his horn becomes worn down to a flat plate as seen above. The two-horned African creature leaves his horns alone. Rhinoceroses are the only known animals, living today, which bear a horn that is solid all through.

"RHINOCEROS UNICORNIS"
(From "Living Animals of the World")

Above is another picture of a Great Indian Rhinoceros. Notice the long and nearly straight horn on his face. This photograph was found in an encyclopedia of wildlife — between the text of an article entitled "Horns of Beauty and Horns of Strength," by Frank Finn. This renowned author of "Wild Animals of Yesterday," says that "of the hoofed animals whose hoofs are not cloven, the rhinoceros is the only one possessing a horn," — they have odd-toed feet with three digits encased in separate hoofs instead. Also, he says some horses have protrusions that suggest they might once have had horns. This should be of particular interest to those who are interested in Darwin's theory of evolution, and also to those who want to believe that the type of unicorn which our forefathers displayed on the Royal Arms or official seal of Great Britain, now the United kingdom, really existed at one time. He points out:

It is a curious fact that in rare cases the horse, presumably as a legacy from the past, shows a tendency to develop them, two bony bosses appearing on the forehead under the skin. But this development, if it proceeded further, would result in the formation of a different type of horn from that of the rhinoceros.

The rhinoceros was never seen by Edward Topsell, for he writes: "The beast is strange and never seen in our country." But he did not need firsthand knowledge of a one-horned creature to present his case for the existence of the unicorn. He maintained that "the Hebrew names in Scripture prove Unicorns," and the following discourse from his work on quadrupeds spells out the evidence. He says:

But to the purpose that there is such a beast, the Scripture itself witnesseth, for David thus speaketh in the 92. Psalm: "Et erigetur cornu meum tanquam Monocerotis." That is, my horn shall be lifted up like the horn of a Unicorn; whereupon all Divines that ever wrote have not only collected that there is a Unicorn, but also affirm the similitude to be betwixt the kingdom of David and the horn of the Unicorn, that as the horn of the Unicorn is wholesome to all beasts and creatures, so should the kingdom of David be in the generation of Christ. And do we think that David would compare the virtue of his kingdom, and the powerful redemption of the world unto a thing that is not, or is uncertain and fantastical? God forbid that ever any wise man should so spite the holy Ghost. For this cause also we read in "Suidas," that good men which worship God and follow his laws, are compared to Unicorns, whose greater parts as their whole bodies are unprofitable and untamable, yet their horn maketh them excellent: so in good men, although their fleshy parts be good for nothing and fall down to earth, yet their grace and piety exalteth their souls to the heavens.

We have shewed already in the story of the Rhinoceros, that "Reem" in Hebrew signifieth a Unicorn, although Munster be of another opinion, yet the Septuagints in the translation of Deut. 33. do translate it a Unicorn.... Rabbi Solamon, David Kimbi, and Saadius always take "Reem" & "Karas" for a Unicorn, and they derive "Reem" from "Rom," which signifieth "Altitudinem" height, because the Horn of the Unicorn is lifted on high. Hereunto the Arabians agree

which call it "Barkeron," and the Persians "Bark."
The Chaldeans "Remana." In the 39. of Job, the Lord
speaketh in this manner to Job . . . . That is to say,
will the Unicorn rest and serve thee, or tarry beside
thy cratches? Canst thou bind the Unicorn with a hal-
ter to thy plow to make furrows, or will he make plain
the clots of the valleys? Likewise in the prophecy
of Isaiah the 34. chap. and in many other places of
Scripture, whereby God himself must needs be tra-
duced, if there be no Unicorn in the world.

Besides the Arabians, as And. Bellun. writeth, call
this beast "Alcherceden," and say that it hath one
horn in the forehead which is good against poisons.
The Graetians call it "Monokeros," from whence Pliny
and all the ancient Grammarians do call it "Monoceros," yet the divines both elder and later do name
it by a more learned proper Latin word "Vnicornis."
The Italians "Alicorno," "Vnicorno," "Liocorno,"
"Leocorne," the French "Licorne," the Spaniards
"Vnicornio," the Germans "Einhorne," the Illirians
"Gednorozeez": And thus much for the name. All our
European Authors which write of beasts, do make of
the Unicorn divers kinds, especially Pliny, Ludoui-
cus Romanus, Paulus Venetus, Nicholous Venetus,
Aeneas Sylvius, Albertus Magnus, out of whose words
we must gather the best description that we can of
the Unicorn.

So, we see from this excerpt there are "divers kinds"
of unicorns — even today, like we have already seen on
the past few pages. Topsell had never seen many of the
creatures he wrote about. His most powerful proof for
the existence of unicorns stood with the evidence in the
Greek Septuagint, which uniformly translated the Hebrew
word "Reem" into "Monoceros," which went into Latin and
the Roman Catholic Latin Vulgate Bible as "unicornis,"
and which eventually went into English as "unicorn."
He published his work four years before the first printing of the renowned King James Authorized Translation
of the Bible, which uniformly used the word "unicorn,"
which, once again, simply means "one-horned."

"Although three and a half centuries have passed since the King James Version was first printed," says Dr. M. W. Smith, "it is still the most widely read book in the world. More copies of the King James Version have been printed than of any other version of the Bible, ancient or modern; indeed, more copies of the King James Version have been printed than of any other book of any nature whatsoever. The passing of time has not lessened its importance or dimmed its luster. It was a copy of the King James Version which William Cowper, the poet, had before him when he penned the hymn-lines:"

"A glory gilds the sacred page,
Majestic, like the sun:
It gives a light to every age;
It gives, but borrows none."

This is an important observation because it is the one book that has had an overwhelming influence in sustaining the belief in the unicorn—in England, Scotland, America, and throughout the rest of the British Empire.

"Perhaps in Scotland more thoroughly than in any other part of the British Empire," says Historiographer Royal for Scotland, J. H. Burton, "the 'authorised version' has been exclusively reverence as the only true version —as the Bible itself."

"The first New Testament printed in America," says People's Cyclopedia "was the Authorized Version, Boston, 1742. The first Bible printed in America was the Authorized Version, 1752; the first Bible printed in America, and having 'an American Imprint,' was the Authorized Version, Philadelphia, 1782."

In spite of the fact that the King, Church, and Parliament officially re-authorized the use of the King James Translation of the Bible in 1662—after the Monarchy was restored—Dr. Thomas Fuller, the author of "The Church History of Britain," who we quoted describing unicorn horns in the last chapter, didn't believe in unicorns, even though the Bible shows they existed. The spirit of skepticism, then as today, played in the minds of religious leaders, and he was not immune to the negative influence of his colleagues. "The plain truth is," he admitted, "I, who first questioned whether there were any unicorns, am since convinced that there are so many sorts of them: the Indian ox, the Indian ass, the oryx, &c. famous for carrying one horn." But what finally convinced him? In referring to the King James Bible, he gives us some clues in the following notice:

> It is uncivil to give the lie to a common tradition, the former existence of such a creature (and surely no species is wholly lost) is cleared from several places of Scripture: "God hath as it were the strength of an unicorn." "Will the unicorn be willing to serve thee?" "My horn shalt thou exalt like the horn of an unicorn," &c. True it is, the word in the original importeth nothing of any horn therein (as doth the Latin "unicornis," and the Greek "monoceros"). Yet I am confident it is rightly rendered, because it is so rendered; such was the learning and piety of the persons employed in that translation.

Notice that Dr. Fuller used the word "translation" — and not version. There is no authorized version, even though Encyclopedia Britannica admits that the English Bible "is now recognized as the 'Authorized Version' wherever the English Language is spoken." "Version" is an absolute misnomer. "The Epistle Dedicatorie" of the original 1611 Bible speaks of an "exact Translation of the holy Scriptures into the English tongue." It says "Translation" — not Version. The highest church official in England, Archbishop Laud, spoke, not of a version, but of "the Translation of King James" when he wrote that it was "named once for all."
And Archbishop Spotswood confirms the high opinion Dr. Fuller had of the translators of that Bible, as well as of good King James, "the Lord's Anointed," who firmly stood behind it. After "a proposition was made for a new translation of the Bible" in Scotland, back in 1601, he says that "His majesty did urge it earnestly, and with many reasons did persuade the undertaking of the work, showing the necessity and profit of it." Nevertheless,

it wasn't done. "Yet did not the king let this his intention fall to the ground," says the Prelate of Scotland, "but after his happy coming to the crown of England set the most learned divines of that Church a-work for the translation of the Bible; which, with great pains and to the singular profit of the Church, they perfected."

The King James Translation of the Bible was proposed at the Hampton Court Conference in 1604, but was not ready for publication until seven years later. "No real opposition was offered to the proposal," says the Encyclopedia Britannica, "and the King cleverly sketched out on the moment a plan to be adopted. He wished that some special pains should be taken in that behalf for one uniform translation — professing that he could never yet see a Bible well translated in English — and this to be done by the best learned in both Universities; after them to be reviewed by the bishops and the chief learned of the Church; from them to be presented to the privy council; and lastly to be ratified by his royal authority; and so this whole church to be bound unto it, and none other."

The Bible was based, in part, on the Septuagint. In her popular work on the famous unicorn tapestries, Margaret B. Freeman says a group of Hebrew scholars in Alexandria were "familiar with the unicorn and were responsible, in effect, for putting him in the Bible. These scholars — tradition says they numbered seventy-two — translated the Old Testament from Hebrew into Greek in about the third to second centuries B. C. In this translation, the Septuagint, the beast called in Hebrew 're êm' became 'monoceros,' that is, unicorn. Modern scholars have pointed out the 're êm' should be identified as the wild ox, but it has remained the unicorn for many centuries. Like the original books of the Old Testament, the Septuagint was considered to be divinely inspired, hence it appeared obvious that the unicorn was authenticated by God himself."

APPENDIX

Since the Hebrews are often mentioned in this work, a synopsis of their history should benefit those not very familiar with the people, places, and events previously touched on. The following topics are some lightly edited excerpts from a well written edition of P. V. N. Myers's "General History for Colleges and High Schools":

THE HEBREWS

The Patriarchal Age. —— Hebrew history begins with the departure of Abraham out of Ur of the Chaldees, about 2000 B.C. The story of Abraham and his nephew Lot, of Isaac and his sons Jacob and Esau, of the sojourn of the descendants of Jacob in Egypt, of the Exodus, of the conquest of Canaan and the apportionment of the land among the twelve tribes of Israel,—— all this marvellous story is told in the Hebrew Scriptures with a charm and simplicity that have made it the familiar possession of childhood.

The Judges (from about 1300 to 1095 B.C.). —— A long period of anarchy and dissension followed the conquest and settlement of Canaan by the Hebrews. "There was no king in Israel: every man did that which was right in his own eyes." During this time there arose a line of national heroes, such as Gideon, Jephthah, and Samson, whose deeds of valor and daring, and the timely deliverance they wrought for the tribes of Israel from their foes, caused their names to be handed down with grateful remembrance to following ages.

These popular leaders were called Judges because they usually exercised judicial functions, acting as arbiters between the different tribes, as well as between man and man. Their exploits are narrated in the Book of Judges, which is a collection of the fragmentary, yet always interesting, traditions of this early and heroic period of the nation's life. The last of the Judges was Samuel, whose life embraces the close of the anarchical age and the beginning of the monarchy.

Founding of the Hebrew Monarchy (about 1095 B.C.). —— During the period of the Judges, the tribes of Israel were united by no central government. Their union was nothing more than a league, or confederation, which has been compared to the Saxon Heptarchy in England. But the common dangers to which they were exposed from the attacks of the half-subdued Canaanitish tribes about them, and the example of the great kingdoms of Egypt and Assyria, led the people to begin to think of the advantages of a closer union and a stronger government. Consequently the republic or confederation was changed into a kingdom, and Saul, of the tribe of Benjamin, a man chosen in part because of his commanding stature and royal aspect, was made king of the new monarchy (about 1095 B.C.).

The king was successful in subduing the enemies of the Hebrews, and consolidated the tribes and settled the affairs of the new state. But towards the close of his reign, his reason became disturbed: fits of gloom and despondency passed into actual insanity, which clouded the closing years of his life. At last he and his three sons fell in battle with the Philistines upon Mount Gilboa (about 1055 B.C.).

The Reign of David (about 1055–1015 B.C.). —— Upon the death of Saul, David, son of Jesse, of the tribe of Judah, who had been previously anointed and encouraged to expect the crown by the prophet Samuel, assumed the scepter. This warlike king transformed the pastoral and half-civilized tribes into a conquering people, and, in imitation of the monarchs of the Nile and the Euprhrates, extended the limits of his empire in every direction, and waged wars of extermination against the troublesome tribes of Moab and Edom.

Poet as well as warrior, David enriched the literature of his own nation and of the world with lyric songs that breathe such a spirit of devotion and trust that they have been ever since his day the source of comfort and inspiration to thousands. He had in mind to build at Jerusalem, his capital city, a magnificent temple, and spent the latter years of his life in collecting material for this purpose. In dying, he left the crown to Solomon, his youngest son, his eldest, Absalom, having been slain in a revolt against his father, and the second, Adonijah, having been excluded from the succession for a similar crime.

APPENDIX

The Reign of Solomon (about 1015-975 B.C.). — Solomon did not possess his father's talent for military affairs, but was a liberal patron of architecture, commerce, and learning. He erected, with the utmost magnificence of adornment, the temple at Jerusalem, planned by his father David. King Hiram of Tyre, who was a close friend of the Hebrew monarch, aided him in this undertaking by supplying him with the celebrated cedar of Lebanon, and with Tyrian architects, the most skilled workmen at that time in the world. The dedication ceremonies upon the completion of the building were most imposing and impressive. Thenceforth this temple was the center of the Jewish worship and of the national life.

For the purpose of extending his commerce, Solomon built fleets upon the Mediterranean and the red Sea. The most remote regions of Asia and Africa were visited by his ships, and their rich and wonderful products made to contribute to the wealth and glory of his kingdom.

Solomon maintained one of the most magnificent courts ever held by an oriental sovereign. When the Queen of Sheba, attracted by the reports of his glory, came from Southern Arabia to visit the monarch, she exclaimed, "The half was not told me." He was the wisest king of the East. His proverbs are famous specimens of sententious wisdom. He was versed, too, in botany, being acquainted with plants and trees "from the hyssop upon the wall to the cedar of Lebanon."

But wise as was Solomon in his words, his life was far from being either admirable or prudent. In conformity with Asiatic custom, he had many wives — seven hundred, we are told — of different nationalities and religions. Through their persuasion the old monarch himself fell into idolatry, which turned from him the affections of his best subjects, and prepared the way for the dissensions and wars that followed his death.

The Division of the Kingdom (about 975 B.C.). — The reign of Solomon was brilliant, yet disastrous in the end to the Hebrew monarchy. In order to carry on his vast undertakings, he had laid most oppressive taxes upon his people. When Rehoboam, his son, succeeded to his father's place, the people entreated him to lighten the taxes that were making their very lives a burden. Influenced by young and unwise counselors, he replied to the petition with haste and insolence: "My father," said he, "chastised you with whips, but I will chastise you with scorpions." Immediately all the tribes, save Judah and Benjamin, rose in revolt, and succeeded in setting up, to the north of Jerusalem, a rival kingdom, with Jeroboam as its first king. This northern state, with Samaria as its capital, became known as the Kingdom of Israel; the southern, of which Jerusalem remained the capital, was called the Kingdom of Judah.

Thus was torn in twain the empire of David and Solomon. United, the tribes might have maintained an empire capable of offering successful resistance to the encroachments of the powerful and ambitious monarchs about them. But now the land becomes an easy prey to the spoiler. It is henceforth the pathway of the conquering armies of the Nile and the Euphrates. Between the powerful monarchies of these regions, as between an upper and nether millstone, the little kingdoms are destined, one after the other, to be ground to pieces.

The Kingdom of Israel (975?-722 B.C.). —— The kingdom of the Ten Tribes maintained an existence for about two hundred and fifty years. Its story is instructive and sad. Many passages of its history are recitals of the struggles between the pure worship of Jehovah and the idolatrous service of the deities introduced from the surrounding nations. The cause of the religion of Jehovah, as the tribes of Israel had received it from the patriarch Abraham and the lawgiver Moses, was boldly espoused and upheld by a line of the most remarkable teachers and prophets produced by the Hebrew race, among whom Elijah and Elisha stand pre-eminent.

The little kingdom was at last overwhelmed by the Assyrian power. In 722 B.C., Sargon, king of Nineveh, took Samaria and carried away the Ten Tribes into captivity beyond the Tigris river. The larger part of the captives were scattered among the Median towns, where they became so mingled with the native population as to be inquired after even to this day as the "lost tribes."

The country, left nearly vacant by this wholesale deportation of its inhabitants, was then filled with other subjects or captives of the Assyrian king. The descendants of these, mingled with the few Jews of the poorer class that were still left in the country, formed the Samaritans of the New Testament-time of the Lord Jesus Christ.

Sargon was a famous builder. Near the foot of the Persian hills he founded a large city, which he named for himself; and there he erected a royal residence, described in the inscriptions as "a palace of incomparable magnificence," the site of which is now preserved by the vast mounds of Khorsabad.

Sennacherib (705-681 B.C.).—— Sennacherib, the son of Sargon, came to the throne 705 B.C. We must accord to him the first place of renown among all the great names of the Assyrian Empire. His name, connected as it is with the story of the Jews, and with many of the most wonderful discoveries among the ruined palaces of Nineveh, has become as familiar to the ear as that of Nebuchadnezzar in the story of Babylon.

The fullness of the royal inscriptions of this reign enables us to permit Sennacherib to tell us in his own words of his great works and military expeditions. Respecting the decoration of Nineveh, he says: "I raised again all the edifices of Nineveh, my royal city; I reconstructed all its old streets, and widened those that were too narrow. I have made the whole town a city of shining like the sun."

Concerning an expedition against Hezekiah, king of Judah, he says: "I took forty-six of his strong fenced cities; and of the smaller towns which were scattered about I took and plundered a countless number. And from these places I captured and carried off as spoil 200,150 people, old and young, male and female, together with horses and mares, asses and camels, oxen and sheep, a countless multitude. And Hezekiah himself I shut up in Jerusalem, his capital city, like a bird in a cage, building towers round the city to hem him in, and raising banks of earth against the gates, to prevent escape."

While Sennacherib was besieging Jerusalem, the king of Egypt appeared in the field in the south with aid for

Hezekiah. This caused Sennacherib to draw off his forces from the siege to meet the new enemy; but near the frontiers of Egypt the Assyrian host, according to the Hebrew account, was smitten by "the angel of the Lord," and the king returned with a shattered army and without glory to his capital, Nineveh.

Sennacherib employed the closing years of his reign in the digging of canals, and in the erection of a splendid palace at Nineveh. He was finally murdered by his sons.

Nabopolassar (625-604 B.C.). — Nabopolassar was the first king of what's called the New Babylonian Monarchy. When troubles and misfortunes began to thicken about the last Assyrian king, Saracus, he entrusted to the care of Nabopolassar, as his viceroy, the towns and provinces of the South. The chance now presented of obtaining a crown proved too great a temptation for the satrap's fidelity to his master. He revolted and became independent in 625 B.C. Later, he entered into an alliance with the Median king, Cyaxares, against his former sovereign. Through the overthrow of Nineveh and the break-up of the Assyrian Empire, the new Babylonian kingdom received large accessions of territory.

Nebuchadnezzar (604 - 561 B.C.). — Nabopolassar was followed by his renowned son Nebuchadnezzar, whose oppressive wars and gigantic architectural works rendered Babylon at once the scourge and the wonder of the ancient world.

The Kingdom of Judah (975?-586 B.C.). — This little kingdom, torn by internal religious dissensions, as was its rival kingdom of the north, and often on the very verge of ruin from Egyptian or Assyrian armies, maintained an independent existence for about four centuries. During this time, a line of kings, of the most diverse character, sat upon the throne. Upon the extension of the power of Babylon to the west, Jerusalem was forced to acknowledge the suzerainty of the Babylonian kings.

The kingdom at last shared the fate of its northern rival. Jerusalem, having repeatedly revolted, was finally taken and sacked. Nebuchadnezzar, in revenge for the uprising of the Jews, had besieged and captured Jerusalem, and carried away a large part of the people, and their king Zedekiah, into captivity at Babylon. The temple was stripped of its sacred vessels of silver and gold, which were carried away to Babylon, and the temple itself with the adjoining palace was delivered to the flames; the people, save a miserable remnant, were also borne away into the "Great Captivity" (586 B.C.).

This event virtually ended the separate and political life of the Hebrew race. Henceforth Judah constituted simply a province of the empires — Babylonian, Persian, Macedonian, and Roman — which successively held sway over the regions of Western Asia, with, however, just one flicker of national life under the Maccabees, during a part of the two centuries preceding the birth of Jesus.

The Fall of Babylon. — In 555 B.C., Nabonadius, the last king of Babylon, began his reign. He seems to have associated with himself in the government his son Belshazzar, who shared with his father the duties and royal honors, apparently on terms of equal co-sovereignty.

To the east of the valley of the Tigris and the Euphrates, beyond the ranges of the Zargos, there had been growing up an Aryan kingdom, the Medo-Persian, which, at the time now reached by us, had excited by its aggressive spirit the alarm of all the nations of Western Asia. For purposes of mutual defense, the king of Babylon, and Croesus, the well-known monarch of Lydia, a state of Asia Minor, formed an alliance against Cyrus, the strong and ambitious sovereign of the Medes and Persians. This league awakened the resentment of Cyrus, and, after punishing Croesus and depriving him of his kingdom, he collected his forces to chastise the Babylonian king.

Anticipating the attack, Nabonadius had strengthened the defenses of Babylon, and stationed around it supporting armies. But he was able to avert the fatal blow for only a few years. Risking a battle in the open field, his army was defeated, and the gates of the capital were thrown open to the Persians (538 B.C.).

With the fall of Babylon, the scepter of dominion, borne for so many years by Semitic princes, was given into the hands of the Aryan peoples, who were destined, from this time forward, to shape the course of events, and control the affairs of civilization.

APPENDIX

Upon the capture of Babylon by the Persian king Cyrus, that monarch, who was kindly disposed towards the Jews that he there found captives, permitted them to return to Jerusalem and restore the temple. Jerusalem thus became again the center of the old Hebrew worship, and, although shorn of national glory, continued to be the sacred center of the ancient faith till the second generation of Christ. Then, in chastisement for repeated revolts, the city was laid in ruins by the Romans.

After one of the most harassing sieges recorded in history, Jerusalem, the holy city, was taken by Titus, son of the Roman Emperor Vespasian (about 70 A.D.). The temple was destroyed, and more than a million of Jews that were crowded in the city are believed to have perished. Great multitudes suffered death by crucifixion. The miserable remnants of the nation were scattered all over the world. Josephus, the great historian, accompanied the conqueror to Rome. In imitation of Nebuchadnezzar, Titus robbed the temple of its sacred utensils, and bore them away as trophies. Upon the triumphal arch at Rome that bears his name may be seen at the present day the sculptured representation of the golden candlestick, which was one of the memorials of war.

In the year 131, the Jews in Palestine, who had in a measure recovered from the blow Titus had given their nation, broke out in desperate revolt, because of the planting of a Roman colony upon the almost desolate site of Jerusalem, and the placing of the statue of Jupiter in the Holy Temple. More than half a million of Jews perished in the useless struggle, and the survivors were driven into exile — the last dispersion of the race.

So, by a series of unparalleled calamities and persecutions, Abraham's descendants were "sifted among all nations"; but to this day they cling with a strange devotion and loyalty to the simple faith of their fathers.

AN ILLUSTRATED COMMENTARY

THE TRUE BIBLICAL UNICORNS

"My horn shalt thou exalt like the horn of an unicorn," — Ps. 92:10. Notice the "2:1" ratio in the Scripture-number — just a coincidence?

"In Ps. xcii. 10," says Dr. Robinson, "which is referred to above as proving that the 'reem' is sometimes represented as having but 'one' horn, the Hebrew reads simply, 'My horn shalt thou exalt like an unicorn,' where the word 'horn,' as it stands in the English version, is no where expressed; although there is undoubtedly an ellipsis." He implies that somewhere he might be specifically represented as having more than one horn. The place would be in Deuteronomy 33:17, where it says "his horns are like the horns of unicorns." The original Hebrew word is apparently "unicorn" (singular); so in this case, he may have had more than one horn. But maybe for the ease of understanding, the King James translators thought it wise to preserve continuity; so they rendered "reem" here in the "collective" sense. The King James Bible we have at hand affirms it is singular (in a note on the same page as the verse). And the words "the horn," underlined above, are in italic letters that show that they were not in the original Hebrew. All of this just adds wonderfully to what we are shortly about to find out.

For the Black Obelisk we have still not been able to acquire a cuneiform transliteration, but the Rev. Dr. Scheil provides the following translation of the epitaph for the central row of reliefs, one of which is shown on the next page. It comes from Vol. IV, p. 52 of a reprinted 1888 edition of "Records of the Past" — six volumes of English translations of the ancient monuments of Egypt and Western Asia, collected, edited, and often done by the Honorable Dr. A. H. Sayce himself:

I have received the tribute of the country of MUTSRI: dromedaries with two humps, an ox of the river SAKEYA (?) an antelope, elephants,* (and) apes "with their young" (?)

Below this translation is the following footnote:

*(Rather "female elephants." Perhaps the next word "baziati" is an adjective in agreement. The "ox" would be either a yak or a rhinoceros according to the bas-relief. — ED.)

The yak is a large wild ox found in the elevated regions of central Asia, and the rhinoceros is not a domesticated animal; so the implication of the translator, by making these propositions, is that the ox is a wild type — the "Rîmu" in Assyrian, or the "Rim," "Reem," "Etc." in Hebrew. Based on these observations, the transliteration of "rîmu" for the wild ox in Hammurabi's Code, and on what "The Illustrated Bible

ONE AND TWO-HORNED UNICORNS AND A FEMALE ANTELOPE
(From the Celebrated Assyrian Black (Basalt) Obelisk)

Dictionary" declares, we can reasonably conclude, without a transliteration of the text on hand, that the Assyrian word for this "ox" is, in
fact, "rîmu." The translated word order is "ox" and then "antelope."
The first two animals, on the left, are quite obviously not antelopes,
but the third is easily recognized as such; so we have only one name,
"rîmu," with which to identify both the one and the two-horned wild ox-
like creatures; so both must have been called "rîmus" in olden times,
or "reemim," as the Hebrews might prefer. Going by the number of horns
on each, the translator must have meant to identify the first creature
as the two-horned yak and the second as the one-horned Indian rhinoceros, but neither of the above have features that really match either
of his choices; and the Assyrians probably had two entirely different
words for these odd creatures anyway. This still leaves us with just
the word "rîmu" or "unicorn" to call either animal—regardless of the
number of horns he might bear. So if "rîmu" is used to identify either
a one or two-horned wild ox-like creature like the above (and they are
nearly identical otherwise); then the biblical unicorn could well have
had up to two horns, and still be the Greek "monoceros," or "unicorn."

Dr. Scheil makes it obvious that the Assyrian "Rîmu" or Hebrew "Reem"
or "Rim" could be a multi-horned animal. He was closely related, or,
even more likely, of exactly the same breed since the Assyrian artist
only employed one word to describe both animals. Except for the horns
and added decorations, they are almost identical; so they are probably
the same breed. One might, per chance, be born with one horn, another
with two. Why class them with two different names? This conclusion is
supported by the fact that the other ancient monuments show them with
both single and double horns, and varying decorations, but portray
them as very similar creatures otherwise. (See Dr. Lübke's drawings:
a - the bull, and d - the unicorn, on p. 88.) In fact, since the Persian
bulls and unicorns look so much alike, in his "Five Great Monarchies,"

Micah v. 7.

" And the remnant of Jacob shall be among the Gentiles in the midst of many people as a LION *among the beasts of the forest, as a* YOUNG LION *among the flocks of sheep : who, if he go through, both treadeth down and teareth in pieces, and none can deliver."*

Deut. xxxiii. 17.

" His glory is like the firstling of his bullock, and his horns like the HORNS OF UNICORNS *: with them he shall push the people together to the* ENDS *of the* EARTH."

Rawlinson repeatedly calls these one-horned animals "half-Bulls." Other prominent writers identify them as "demi-bulls." So all of this strongly supports our conclusion that the one and two-horned wild bulls or bullocks of Assyria and Persia, and nearby Palestine alike, were almost certainly the unicorns spoken of in the Bible. The Hebrews knew this, and made it very clear in Psalm 92:10 and Deuteronomy 33:17.

The latter is inscribed above, under the charging unicorns. Both sprang from the two-horned bullock (rîmu)——a symbol for all Israel. They eventually migrated west, across Europe, to the British Isles, to be promptly venerated on the Scottish Royal Arms; but later they parted company: one galloped off to England to be heralded on the Royal Arms of Great Britain; the other sailed to America to be proclaimed on the Great Seals of Virginia, New York, and all of New England. (See page 83. In a future work on Unicorns and the Whirlwind, we hope to expand much more on the subject. Meanwhile, relevant reading material can be obtained from Artisan Sales, in Thousand Oaks, California.)

They say a picture is worth a thousand words. It's true! If the old Assyrian Standard from Khorsabad, illustrated on the following page, is studied and very carefully compared to the appropriate Scriptures, prophetic truths will abundantly manifest themselves. Space prevents a detailed explanation here, but a few clues can spur an inquiry: Jonah converted Nineveh, and he certainly preached the Scriptures, because this handsome Assyrian standard portrays many Hebrew prophecies like Deut. 33:17, and the blessings recorded in Genesis 48:19-20——for the

AN ASSYRIAN STANDARD.

half-tribes of Ephraim and Manasseh. The two unicorns are born from the split head (and horns) of the bullock, or "rîmu." Ps. 22:21 is also portrayed therein: Save me from the lion's mouth: for thou hast heard me from the horns of the unicorns." Notice Job's God standing above the whirlwind flowing as rivers of living water——NE, and NW to the Isles. "Behold," says Jeremiah, "the whirlwind of the LORD goeth forth with fury." On the head of the God shooting forth his arrows is the "Fleur-de-lis," or Cross, symbolizing the Trinity or Jesus Christ. And He, as The Word, Rimmon, the Unicorn, the Rock and Horn of our Salvation, migrated from Israel, through Europe, and finally to Great Britain. "Hear the word of the LORD, O ye nations," says Jeremiah, "and declare it in the isles afar off." There the Horn of the Unicorn was exalted to its highest. Shepard says: "Ctesias gives the length of the horn as one cubit or eighteen inches, Aelian as a cubit and a half, Pliny as two cubits, Solinus and Isidore as four feet, Cardan as three cubits, Rebelais as six or seven feet, and Albertus Magnus as ten feet"——and it reached its maximum length during Topsell's time, when the King James Bible was being translated. And as more self-appointed versions

A FLEMISH BOOK OF HOURS MADE FOR JAMES IV (C. 1505)

issue forth, it grows shorter and shorter. Notice the stub sprouting from the head of the Unicorn on the Royal Arms of Great Britain today!

The red haired Scottish kings, who meticulously traced their bloodline back to ruddy old Adam, knew the religious significance of unicorns. Above we see King James IV bowed down and worshipping before two unicorns looking to the front and rear on the Royal Scottish Arms. They appear to be embroidered on the altar frontal of the Royal Chapel.

"The unicorn is a familiar symbol of our Lord Jesus Christ," says F. R. Webber, "From the center of his forehead rises a great spiral horn. It is a symbol of our Lord's Incarnation and His sinless life." In his work "Church Symbolism," he adds: "Among the many notable examples of the unicorn as a symbol of our Saviour we might mention those to be seen in the form of carvings or paintings at Strasbourg Cathedral, at the famous Grimmenthal Church, now destroyed, on the doors of Pisa, at Lyons, Toledo, St. Sebald's at Nuremberg, St. Botolph's at Boston, at Erfurt, Bourges, Beverley, Lincoln, Ely, Chester and Manchester."

Odell Shepard speaks of a "beautiful painting of the Madonna and Child by Stefan Lochner in the Wallraf-Richartz Museum at Cologne. On the Madonna's bosom there is a large jewelled brooch which shows in the middle a seated maiden with a unicorn resting in her lap." "Our Lord Jesus Christ, the spiritual unicorn, descended into the womb of the Virgin and through her took on human flesh. He was captured by the Jews and condemned to die on the cross," states an old Latin "Physiologus." "The one horn that he has on his head signifies the words of the Savior: 'I and my Father are one.'"

The Persian Scriptures make it clear the ancient Aryans worshipped "that sacred beast the Unicorn" (Jesus), and a noted Anglican bishop, Jeremy Taylor, devoutly wrote, in defense of his religion, to a Roman Catholic gentleman: "We speak honorably of His most Holy Name. We worship Him at the mention of His Name"——not the symbolic Unicorn, but the precious Name of "Jesus" instead. But sadly, this is no longer the case; and what follows affirms it. Because today most Christians have no easy access to this rare and intentionally neglected historical information, it is relevant, appropriate, and a duty for us to bring these obscure facts to light again. We begin with an 1883 definition:

"**Bowing, in the Creed.** A reverent act of worship at the Name of Jesus (Phil. ii. 10)," write the Laity of the Protestant Episcopal Church in their 'Church Cyclopaedia.' "The text upon which this bowing is based refers properly to a bending of the knee, which was an Oriental act of homage. It is only when His Name, JESUS, is uttered that this reverent bowing is proper, JESUS is His Name as man with us. CHRIST is His title, as anointed to His threefold office as Prophet, Priest, and King. Therefore St. Paul's arguments with the Thessalonians were accurately stated, 'that this JESUS whom I proclaim unto you is the CHRIST.' The 18th Canon of the Church of England makes bowing at the Name of JESUS proper, not only in the Creed, but at all other times when It is mentioned. 'When, in time of Divine service, the LORD JESUS shall be mentioned, due and lowly reverence shall be done by all persons present as hath been accustomed: testifying by these outward ceremonies and gestures their inward humility, Christian resolution, and due acknowledgment that the LORD JESUS CHRIST, the true eternal SON of GOD, is the only Saviour of the world, in whom alone all the mercies, graces, and promises of GOD to mankind for this life and the life to come are fully and wholly comprised.' (Canons of 1603 A.D.)"

The proud Puritan preachers hated to teach this humble reverence for their Savior's Name, and they vehemently refused to bend a knee to "the sweet sound of Jesus." One of the particulars of the infamous Millenary Petition that they presented to James I in 1603 insisted "that ministers may not be charged to teach their people to bow at the name of Jesus." How could they claim Him as their Master and not bow to His precious Name? Needless to say, that "religious king" cast their blasphemous plea back down into the bottomless pit whence it had wormed its way up, and he promptly made the 18th Canon one of the laws of the land. "The king, in his ratification of these canons," wrote the old Puritan historian Daniel Neal, "commands them to be diligently observed and executed; and for the better observation of the same, that every parish-minister shall read them over once every year in his church, on a Sunday or holiday, before divine service; and all archbishops, bishops, and others, having ecclesiastical jurisdiction, are commanded to see all and every the same put in execution, and not spare to execute the penalties in them severally mentioned on those that wilfully break or neglect them." "However," says Neal—speaking of the 18th Canon— "no penalty was annexed to the neglect of this ceremony, nor did any suffer for it, till bishop Laud was at the head of the church, who pressed it equally with the rest, and caused above twenty ministers to be fined, censured, and put by their livings, for not bowing at the Name of Jesus, or for preaching against it."

The canons "were passed by the Convocation of Canterbury, and agreed to by the Convocation of York," says Dr. William Boyd Carpenter, "and they were published for the 'due observation of them' by the King's authority under the Great Seal of England." They numbered one hundred and forty, and remained unaltered for two hundred and sixty-two years.

The People's Cyclopedia of Universal Knowledge of 1883 says it was "a custom in the early Christian Church to bow at the Name of Jesus. This is still done in the Church of Rome, at whatever part of the service the Name occurs." Not for long! Lucifer's Pride prevailed. The arrogant Puritans, who eagerly begged in—but never bothered to bow at—the Name of their so-called Master, soon infected their rivals (See Prov. 30:12). Today Catholics also no longer bother to humble themselves, as their grandparents had done so willingly—at the mention of their Savior's Name. The following Roman Catholic testimony is taken from an 1899 edition of "The Catechism Explained, An Exhaustive Exposition of the Christian Religion, with special reference to the present state of society and the spirit of the age." It inadvertently shows the extent, in just 16 years, that the Puritanical persuasion had diminished the orthodox resolve of its Catholic foes to obey a clear-cut biblical precept requiring humbleness at the sound of The Holy Name—JESUS:

Newton, the great astronomer, had the deepest respect for the Name of God; he uncovered his head and bowed low whenever It was uttered in his presence. Many devout Christians bow their head when they pronounce the Name of Jesus in prayer: the priest does so in celebrating Mass. St. Ignatius, Bishop of Antioch, who when a child is said to have been he whom our Lord set in the midst of the disciples, at the time that He said: "Whosoever shall humble himself as this little child, he is the greater in the kingdom of heaven" (Matt. xviii. 4), loved to repeat the Name of Jesus; shortly before his death he said: "This Name shall never leave my lips or be effaced from my heart." And, in fact, after his martyrdom, the holy Name was found inscribed on his heart. In the Litany of the Holy Name we invoke the Name of Jesus again and again, because It is the most powerful of all names, and through It we can obtain all we need. "If you ask the Father anything in My Name, He will give it you" (John xvi. 23). By the Name of Jesus the apostles and saints worked miracles; St. Peter said to the lame man at the gate of the Temple: "In the Name of Jesus Christ arise and walk." (Acts iii. 6). Christ promised that in His Name devils should be cast out (Mark xvi. 17). The devils tremble at the Name of Jesus; they take flight when they hear It, even when It is uttered by evil men, so great is Its potency. The Name of Jesus is also all-powerful to fill the heart with joy; It is compared to oil (Cant. i. 2); as oil gives light, alleviates pain, and affords nourishment, so does the Name of Jesus, when we call upon It. St. Vincent Ferrer declares It to be a defence in all dangers spiritual and temporal, and the means of healing bodily infirmities. All graces are combined in this Holy Name; "There is no other name under heaven given to men, whereby we must be saved" (Acts iv. 12). "At the Name of Jesus every knee should bow, of those that are in heaven, on earth, and under the earth" (Phil. ii. 10).

"I will pour upon the house of David, and upon the inhabitants of Jerusalem," says the LORD, "the spirit of grace and of supplications: and they shall look upon me whom they have pierced, and they shall mourn for him, as one mourneth for his only son, and shall be in bitterness for him, as one that is in bitterness for his firstborn. In that day shall there be a great mourning in Jerusalem, as the mourning of Ha-dad-rim-mon." (Zech. 12:10-11) "Nowack, and others find here the name of a god whose death is lamented," says "A New Standard Bible Dictionary." It is "compounded of two names of divinities."——"Ha-Dad," our heavenly Father, and "Rim-mon"——the Unicorn——His Son: